More Adey - Oscar Wilde's Forgotten Friend

Erratum

Pages 29 and 30 elide two distinct events. The first night of *Lady Windermere's Fan* was on 20th February 1892. Adey's meeting with Aubrey Beardsley had been on the 14th February

More Adey -
Oscar Wilde's Forgotten Friend

by

Michael Seeney

High Wycombe
The Rivendale Press
2017

ISBN 978 1 904201 28 1

Published by

Rivendale Press
P. O. Box 85
High Wycombe
Bucks HP14 4WZ
England

PRINTED AND BOUND BY CPI GROUP (UK) LTD., CROYDON, CR0 4YY

Front cover image: One of a series of photographs of More Adey taken in 1925 by Vyvyan Holland in the garden of Under-the-Hill House. Merlin Holland Collection.

Rear cover image: Aubrey Beardsley frontispiece for *Pastor Sang*.

CONTENTS

ILLUSTRATIONS

PLATES

WILLIAM MORE ADEY

INTRODUCTION

The phrase "Wilde circle" has been a recognised shorthand from the earliest biographers of Oscar Wilde and historians of the eighteen nineties. Alongside the young men whose presence around Wilde formed the basis of his prosecution for gross indecency, there was a group of artists, writers and aesthetes whose achievements would probably not have sustained the interest of historians and biographers had they not been associated with Wilde. Some, like Aubrey Beardsley and Charles Ricketts would have come to be appreciated for their work no matter what their association. Others, like John Gray or Richard le Gallienne would probably have been relegated to footnotes in histories of the period. The star at the heart of the circle, Lord Alfred Douglas, might not even have written poetry had he not met Wilde but, whatever his own view of its merits his verse is not the reason he is remembered today. Robert Ross's position in this historical circle is well summed up in the title of Margery Ross's compilation of his letters, *Robert Ross: Friend of Friends*. Ross lives on through the memories and achievements of others: his own literary output was meagre; he painted no pictures, produced no plays but he was the great arranger, introducer and stimulus for others.

But all these people did play a part in the Oscar Wilde story, and that is the main reason why there are biographies of them; in some cases more biographies than – as Lady Bracknell would say – "statistics have lain down for our guidance". At Wilde's funeral Robert Ross placed a wreath of laurels inside which he inscribed the names of "those who had shown kindness to him during or after his imprisonment"; they were: Arthur Humphreys, Max Beerbohm, Arthur Clifton, Ricketts, Shannon, Conder, Rothenstein, Dal Young, Mrs Leverson, More Adey, Alfred Douglas, Reginald Turner, Frank Harris, Louis Wilkinson, Mellor, Miss Schuster, Rowland Strong and C[arlos] B[lacker]. One name on this list that has received almost no attention to date is More Adey. Look him up in the index to Richard Ellmann's *Oscar Wilde* and he does not make an appearance until page 437; there are four fleeting mentions of him in Hesketh Pearson's biography and yet there are twenty-four letters from Wilde to Adey between September 1896 and April 1900, many of them long. In July 1897 Wilde wrote:

> I had no claim on you, and you have been to me the most wonderful of friends, the most generous, the most forbearing.

And yet if Adey is remembered now it is either for Wilde's description of him as having as much sense as a tom-tit in a hedge, or for meeting Wilde on his release from Pentonville prison and riding with him to Stewart Headlam's home. Where was Adey before Wilde's imprisonment? Where was he after Wilde's death? What short biographical pieces exist about him mention that he spent the last years of his life in an asylum, but none offers an explanation beyond what Siegfried Sassoon gives in his memoirs – a flawed description of Adey at best.

Like most people who do not live in the public eye, much of Adey's life cannot be known. Unlike most people, the record of a lot of that life appears to have been discarded, wilfully or otherwise when he was removed from the world and placed in the asylum where he spent the last seventeen years of his life. Except for a very few pieces of correspondence preserved by their recipients, only material with a direct relevance to his relationship with Oscar Wilde seems to have survived. Adey was self-effacing – never writing under his own name for example – and modest. Reconstructing such a life is difficult and there remain large areas which are either blank or not easy to understand. His early life is almost entirely undocumented and his time in the asylum is not documented at all except for one official record of him being there in 1939. Although he lived until 1942 he was effectively dead to the world from 1925.

Why write his story, such as it is, now? Because of Wilde's words; because Adey was a companion to Robert Ross for perhaps thirty years; because he was an accomplished art critic, collector, administrator; and because – apart from some hot-headed words of Wilde's about his financial acumen – nobody seems ever to have had a bad word to say about him. He was a good friend to many but remembered by almost none. He lies in an unmarked grave and is seldom more than a footnote in the biographies of other people. I hope that now he will at least have a place in the bibliographies of those biographies and that perhaps there will be a greater understanding of this gentle, modest, friend.

I have been interested in Adey for many years, and it has taken that long to assemble even the amount of material that I include here. Many people have helped, knowingly or unknowingly over that time and some of them are no longer with us. Wilde's life and relationships cannot be understood without reading his letters, and Merlin Holland is, as so many Wildeans recognise, owed a deep debt of gratitude for skilfully editing those letters and for giving permission to quote them. He has also generously shared his knowledge of Adey and the photographs which his father took in 1925.

Libraries with Adey collections are few and far between, and pre-eminent among these is the William Andrews Clark Library in Los Angeles where I spent a very happy week wallowing in Adey. The Oxford libraries of University College and Magdalen College have also provided helpful access and considerable material on Adey's relationships with Lord Alfred Douglas and Christopher Millard. The London Library has, as always, given serendipitous insights and loaned books unavailable elsewhere. The British Library's online newspaper archive was not available when I first became interested in Adey and, although his name was not regularly in the press the archive is invaluable in tangential research. The Heritage Centre in Wotton under Edge was an early point of contact and gave me much background on Adey's early life.

Individuals who have provided snippets of material over the years – and I will have forgotten some – include Matthew Sturgis, John Cooper, John Stratford, Sir John Adye, Steven Halliwell, Mark Samuels Lasner, Philip Cohen, Nicholas Frankel, Devon Cox, Barbara Pezzini, Samuel Shaw, The Revd Prebendary Gerard Irvine, Philip Healy, Peter Vernier, Paul Rassam, Joseph Bristow and the people of Wotton under Edge.

1. EARLY LIFE

Wotton-under-Edge is a small rural market town on the edge of the Cotswolds. It stands in Gloucestershire half way between Bristol and Gloucester. Domesday Book valued the town at 60 shillings and by 1538 it was described as "a pratty market town well occupied with clothiers"; the clothiers have gone but it remains one of those essentially honey-coloured towns which draw people to the Cotswolds. For More Adey the town – and more particularly his house in the town – exerted a strong influence throughout his life; he returned there regularly while based in London and retired there for what he no doubt expected would be the rest of his life.

William Moore Adey (Moore was a family name, but he renounced the second "o" as an adult) was born on 22 July 1858. He was the youngest of five children, the other four being girls ranging from four to eleven years old at the time of his birth. Ellen Margaret, the first born in 1847, had been followed at fairly regular intervals by Amy Constance in 1849, Winifred in 1852 and Emma Elizabeth – named after her mother – in 1854. Why Winifred should have been the only child to have been given only one forename is not known.

The Adeys were an old and important family in Gloucestershire. They had been prominent clothiers and mill owners for generations. The first Adey in the records is Morgan Adey who, in 1608 was described as a clothier. His son, the first of a number of Daniel Adeys, took on the lease of Penley's Mill in 1708 as well as owning Knowles Mill outside Wotton. His son, another Daniel, had added another two mills by 1763. This Daniel and his wife Bridget (nee Crew) had six sons and three daughters. The second son, Charles, married twice; his second wife, Sarah Wallington, was the daughter of a "clothier" from Uley, about five miles north east of Wotton and Charles moved there. For the Adey family it was to be a short-lived move; there had been one son from the first marriage (another Daniel) who was described as "of Saddlewood" (between Wotton and Tetbury). This Daniel seems to have been the first Adey to attend university, going up to Oriel College, Oxford in 1741. Another Adey – John, son of Henry – went to Oriel at much the same time but although he was a Gloucestershire Adey, he does not appear to have been close family. Within a generation his descendants had changed their name to Adye. The only son of Charles's second marriage was the first to have Moore in his name – William Moore Adey. He too married twice, both times to daughters of local clothing families. The first marriage, to Sarah Larton, took place in 1794 but there were no children. The second, in 1806, to Emma Austin resulted in two sons. As Emma was from Wotton this was probably when William moved back to the town. By 1824 he was Mayor of Wotton.[1]

William and Emma's first son was also William Moore Adey, born in 1810. He seems to have been the first in the family for over eighty years to go to university, matriculating at Exeter College, Oxford in 1828 and receiving his BA in 1831. The second son, Anthony, was born in 1815. He does not appear to have gone to university, becoming a solicitor in Wotton and Mayor of the town in 1841.

A short walk from the centre of the town on a hill which affords a view of the parish church stands Under-the-Hill House. It isn't clear whether Adey was born in this house; it had been owned by the family since around 1806, but Adey's grandmother Emma passed it to More's father Anthony Adey only in 1867. They had been renting the house for a while before then, but the 1851 census shows the family – with only two daughters by that time – living in Culverhay Rectory House. This property, more properly known at that time as the Old Rectory House (on the road called Culverhay) and later as The Court House, was owned by the Adey family but possibly not until 1873 – there is a gap in the deeds. By 1873 they also owned Edbrooke House. In 1861, by which time the family was complete, the census shows them still in Culverhay, but with the addition of four servants and a governess.

Under-the-Hill House itself started life as a field barn and was turned into a basic house around 1611. In the eighteenth century a new owner, Thomas Rous, added a large number of typically Queen Anne features to the house: elaborate cornicing and dentils carry a wide lead gutter under the eaves; a hipped roof with two large chimneys; two dormer windows facing the church and, most obviously, a bell turret dated 1726. The rope to ring the bell still descends through the house to the bottom of the main stairwell. This galleried staircase was added later in the eighteenth century by the next owners, the Bearpacker family, along with new windows and higher ceilings in the main reception rooms. At this time the house was known as Venn's House, only acquiring the name of Under-the-Hill House during the time the Adeys lived there.

No family seems to have been able to leave the house untouched, and the Adeys introduced oak panelling and window shutters inside; moved the front door from the garden side of the house to its current position alongside the road and extended the drawing room.

In the 1970s a local estate agent listed the house and described it as

> An interesting country property principally of Queen Anne character with several period features including a bell tower dated 1726, situated in a most charming position on the outskirts of the old world country town of Wotton-under-Edge just below the southern escarpment of the Cotswold Hills and about 20 miles by road from the cities of Bath, Bristol and Gloucester.
>
> The house stands 300 feet above sea level on rising ground adjoining Adey's Lane. It is a few minutes' walk only from the centre of the town and enjoys open views to the south and west.

Although the agent's headlines underplay the size of the property, the detailed description includes nine bedrooms (of which three are "staff quarters"), two bathrooms, entrance hall, inner hall, drawing room, dining room, study, kitchen, laundry room and boiler room, as well as a two bedroomed self-contained flat on the first floor.[2]

More Adey's father, Anthony Adey, seems to have had limited historical and artistic interests. When the contents of Under-the-Hill House were auctioned in 1926 there was almost nothing evident of More Adey's interests or personality. The books were good sets of Samuel Johnson, Walter Scott and Thomas Moore; major works on gardening, Bewick's *Birds* and *Quadrupeds* and assorted history, travel and literature. Four lots were simply described as "various books" but the forty or so lots did not add up to much of a library. There were almost no pictures: five anonymous portraits, three paintings on canvas "and another", four Arundel prints and an engraving of a portrait of Joseph Neeld Esq, seated by S Cousins after Archer Shee. These are not the results of a lifetime's collecting by an art critic and connoisseur.

On 23 March 1869, Adey's father Anthony died and Adey was left with a house full of women, including his paternal grandmother, from whom a few years later he was to inherit other property in the town; he didn't inherit the main house until his mother's death in 1900. In the 1861 census there had been five female servants as well.

In 1870 Adey entered the Junior School at Clifton College in Bristol. The school had been founded in 1862 and the extensive site was still being developed throughout Adey's time there. Swimming baths had recently been added, along with a cricket pavilion. In 1870 the library and additional classrooms were built and in 1871 a Physical Laboratory and associated

Fig. 1 The Adey family. A teenaged More Adey is sitting on the floor. The man standing is probably Arthur Turner, husband of Amy Constance Adey.

workshop were erected on the site of a fives court (two new courts were built to replace it) and the following year the new courts were replaced with an open racquet court. Before he left, Adey would also have seen a new organ presented by the Choral Society, a confectioner's shop and various roofings-in and extensions. The most significant change during this period was the building of a separate Junior School in 1876. As the *Clifton College Register* says of this innovation:

> Up to this time the Juniors had been taught in Big-School. What nerves of iron must the Junior School masters have then enjoyed, with five forms taught simultaneously in that School, where every sound echoes and re-echoes! Each master had a bell, which he sounded when he wished to admonish his colleagues that the noise was intolerable, and his own form inaudible. Not infrequently all five bells were sounded at once. Happy, indeed, their release.[3]

In the Junior School, Adey boarded in Poole House, presided over by Rev. R B Poole; when he moved to Big-School he was put in Wiseman's under T W Dunn.

Adey was on the Classical side during his senior years in the college but the archivist could find no reference to him other than the bare essentials in the register. This strongly suggests he didn't excel at sport; indeed, although this may be unfair, it does not appear from the Register that Wiseman's distinguished itself in sport until the years after Adey had left. As at all public schools in the nineteenth century, sport was an important element of the education offered. Two years after Adey's first term, the young Henry John Newbolt came to the school. Many years later – in 1892 - he was to write one of the best known cricketing poems in English – "Vitaï Lampada", which begins, "There's a breathless hush in the Close tonight". The Close was the name of Clifton's sports ground. In the same intake, of September 1876, was Arthur Bellamy Clifton, Adey's future colleague at the Carfax Gallery. Robert Ross had also won a scholarship to Clifton but, for reasons unknown, never took it up.

With the exception of the fagging system and its ilk, boys in different years at public schools will have had little to do with one another but it may be worth noting that among other boys at Clifton at the same time as Adey (although not in the same year) were Roger Fry, with whom he was to lock horns at the Burlington Magazine, and Otho Lloyd, Constance's brother, who arrived only a year after Adey. J E McTaggart, who arrived at Clifton in 1882, was among those approached by Adey when he was seeking financial and moral support for Wilde after his imprisonment; by 1895 Mc Taggart was at Trinity College Cambridge, a member of the Cambridge Apostles and shortly to publish his first book, *Studies in Hegelian Dialectic*; he apparently contributed funds to Adey's collection.

The year before Adey left Clifton the first of his sisters to leave home, Amy Constance, married Arthur Turner. There is some suggestion among local historians that this was a scandal because Turner was a clerk in Anthony Adey's solicitors' office; this may have been the case but it cannot have lasted long as Anthony Adey took him on as a partner. Amy further surrounded Adey with female company by having three daughters in quick succession, but Arthur died in 1888. The following year Constance married again, this time to a bank worker called Walter Samuel Clarke, whose son would eventually inherit on Adey's death.

Notes

1 The history of Wotton under Edge has been told a number of times. I have benefited from reading *Wotton under Edge* by E S Lindley, Museum Press 1962, *Wotton-under-Edge: Time Past-Time Present* by R Perry, the Author 1986, and *Under the Hill* by Simon Herrick, Alan Sutton 1979. I have also visited the town and its Heritage Centre and stayed in Adey's home.

2 At the time of going to press, Under-the-Hill House is for sale for £1.1 million. From the estate agent's brochure it appears that the interior has been considerably altered since I stayed there.

3 *Clifton College Annals and Register 1862-1925*, edited by F Borwick, J W Arrowsmith 1925, p. lxvii

2. KEBLE AND AFTER

On leaving Clifton in 1876 Adey went up to Keble College, Oxford at the start of the Michaelmas term. The architect William Butterfield had caused considerable controversy with his neo-gothic building - its white stripes across a red brick façade standing out against the stone walls of other colleges. It will have reminded Adey of the main building at Clifton College.

The decision to build the new college had only been taken in 1866; money had to be raised, land acquired, a new road built and the college buildings erected, and yet Keble was still able to open to undergraduates in 1870 for an initial intake of thirty one students. By the time Adey arrived the annual intake had reached forty two, and in 1878 the Hall, which can accommodate three hundred, opened.

The proposals for the college provided for each undergraduate room to have a table and three chairs, an elbow or folding chair, a bookcase with cupboards, a carpet, blinds, a stump iron bedstead with straw palliasse mattress, quilt, wool bolster and pillow; a washstand, five pieces of crockery, a goblet and tumbler, looking-glass, chest of drawers, water-can, bath, fire-irons, guard, fender and coal-scuttle.[1]

The first Warden of Keble was Edward Stuart Talbot, whose mother Caroline was the brother of James Stuart-Wortley. His son Archibald became a painter who lived just along the road from the Wildes in Tite Street.[2]

It is not at all clear why Adey chose Keble; his grandfather had been at Exeter College. Wilde's Oxford friend David Hunter-Blair may give us a clue:

> Many men from the first drifted into Keble simply because it was cheap, not because its church discipline appealed to them.[3]

Again, beyond what is published in *Alumni Oxonienses* there is no record of Adey's time here. At school and at Oxford he seems to have kept his head down. But then came the greatest explicit sign of rebellion in his life; in 1879 he converted to Catholicism. This wouldn't have mattered if he had been at any other college, but Keble was an Anglican college and he was forced to leave, having been at the College for only eight terms.

Geoffrey Rowell has said that

> The overriding concern of those behind the founding of Keble was that the college should permanently remain what it was

> intended to be 'in respect of (1) consisting of members of the Church of England only, and (2) providing for them teaching and worship in accordance with its doctrines and Order'[4]

All undergraduates were expected to go to chapel twice on Sundays and to morning chapel 'regularly' during the week. No wonder then that a Catholic convert would not be welcome in the college. The college chapel was only completed in the year Adey went up and was opened on St Mark's Day (25 April).

Adey returned to Oxford to take his BA in 1881 as an unsupported student. His MA followed – as a formality – three years later. Ironically, given his later interests, it was in 1881 that the library of Keble acquired its first mediaeval manuscript and secured over the next twenty years "the most remarkable collection of illuminated manuscripts preserved in an Oxford college library".[5]

He clearly did not keep in touch with his old College: he did not become a member of the Keble Association, and the *Keble Register*, published in 1923 gives his profession as "Holy Orders", a profession he seems never to have contemplated entering.

Catholics had only recently been readmitted to Oxford and their presence remained controversial. But the year before Adey's conversion, on 17 May 1878, the Oxford University Catholic Club had been established, largely as a result of the efforts of Hartwell de la Garde Grisell, who had opened a private oratory at 60 High Street which was frequented by many early converts at the university. Wilde had first met Grisell in Rome, and knew him again in Oxford. In 1900 however, writing to Ross from Rome in April, Wilde said:

> We came to Rome on Holy Thursday ... and yesterday, to the terror of Grissell and all the Papal Court, I appeared in the front rank of the pilgrims in the Vatican, and got the blessing of the Holy Father – a blessing they would have denied me.[6]

In 1893 William Rothenstein published a collection of lithographs called *Oxford Characters*, with each portrait accompanied by a short text. Of Grissell he says:

> Mr Hartwell de la Garde Grissell took his degree in 1865, and is an M.A. upon the books of Brasenose College. He was appointed, after his reception into the Catholic Church, a *Cameriere di Spada e Cappa* to Pius IX; an office which he retains at the court of Leo XIII, and which involves a yearly period of residence in Rome, where he is well known by English

> visitors for his courtesies at the Vatican and elsewhere. He is a Fellow of the Society of Antiquaries of London, a member of the Numismatical Society and also of the Roman Arcadia; and, as these distinctions would imply, he has no slight learning and interest in matters of art, more particularly of art ecclesiastic and Italian. There are many Oxford men, Catholics and otherwise, who have grateful and pleasant memories of their host, and of his treasures, in the house at the High Street end of Long Wall; and, having no official connection with the University, he may be said to represent, in a singular and charming degree, a characteristic side of social academic life in the ancient city.[7]

Perhaps Adey was one of the undergraduates who fell under Grisell's spell. David Hunter Blair says of Grisell

> He was a born collector, and had brought together in his corner-house in the High, masses of curiosities of all kinds, from eggshells and foreign stamps to autograph letters from Saints and Popes, which he hospitably invited all and sundry to come and inspect. At one time he got a perfectly undeserved reputation for clandestinely proselytizing in the interests of Rome; and absurd fables were told of his inviting impressionable undergraduates to dine with him and view his treasures, a wily Jesuit or other subtle ecclesiastic being asked to meet him. Grisell (according to the legend), would presently leave the youth to a tête-à-tête with the emissary of Rome; and the sequel would be, or might be, an appointment at St Aloysius', and a hurried reception into the Catholic Church.[8]

Hunter Blair had himself converted to Catholicism only in 1875.

The University Catholic Club was to meet fortnightly and the rules provided that, at each meeting "a discussion take place on some political or social question of interest to Catholics".[9] Adey is not listed among the members in 1879 but it is more than likely that he would have attended and perhaps gone on to become a member. The Club later became the Newman Society.

The likelihood of Adey's association is strengthened by the coincidence that in 1879 the President of the Club was B F C Costelloe BA of Balliol College. Benjamin Francis Conn Costelloe (always known as Frank) was from an unlikely background: his father was an Irish foreman ship-builder in Glasgow and Frank was clearly adept at winning scholarships which took him first to Glasgow University and then to Oxford in 1874. He had been awarded his BA in 1878 and was called to the Bar in 1881; shortly

Fig. 2 Count Eric Stenbock.

after leaving Oxford he became Count Stenbock's manager. As we shall see, at that time Adey and Stenbock were very close friends.

Other members of the Club included A C Dunlop, who converted to Catholicism while a Magdalen undergraduate and with whom Wilde reported talking "sentimental religion"[10] and Cecil Smyth Pigott, nephew of Edward Smyth Pigott, Examiner of Plays for the Lord Chamberlain, the man who banned Wilde's *Salome* and who was described by Bernard Shaw as "a walking compendium of vulgar insular prejudice".

There were two Catholic places of worship within Oxford: St Aloysius's and St Ignatius's. The former, now the Oxford Oratory on Woodstock Road, had been consecrated in 1875 but by this time the number of converts from Anglicanism earlier in the century had dwindled as the trappings of Ritualism and High Church became more widely available in Anglican churches. Gerard Manley Hopkins, coincidentally back in Oxford in the year of Adey's conversion and a member of the Catholic Club, had said to his father of his own move to Rome, "I am surprised you shd. say fancy and aesthetic tastes have led me to my present state of mind; those wd. be better satisfied in the Church of England, for bad taste is always meeting one in the accessories of Catholicism".[11]

St Aloysius's admirably demonstrated this. As one of Hopkins's biographers has said, "In its bid for respectability in Oxford, St Aloysius's had succeeded only in achieving a dull middle-class sobriety in a building of considerable banality."[12] It suffered from its proximity, and architectural inferiority, to both the Anglican St Barnabas's and Keble College. Nevertheless, Wilde records breakfasting with Father Parkinson, the Superior at St Aloysius's and attending the church.[13]

St Ignatius's in St Clement's was an older establishment and, for Hopkins and for other undergraduates, had a more congenial atmosphere than St Aloysius's. Some undergraduates who attended had not yet converted and going to the little chapel must have seemed a less dramatic statement than attendance at St Aloysius's. This may have been the case for Adey who, despite his love of art and the beautiful seems to have maintained a degree of austerity in his manner of living.

Whether Adey remained in Oxford after his departure from Keble, he certainly visited, and on one of those visits we see the first evidence of his interest in the supernatural. The *Oxford Magazine* in February 1883 reported a meeting of the Phasmatological Society:

> A meeting of this Society was held in Mr A C Headlam's rooms New College, at which 22 members were present. Messrs Bate, Schiller and More Adey introduced stories, which were discussed by the Society, the last being of particular interest.

The Phasmatological Society had been founded in 1878 and the President at this time was the historian Charles Oman. The Society for Psychical Research – the first such society in the world – had been established in 1882, and Oxford was to get its own undergraduate society for Psychical Research which grew out of the Phasmatological Society.

Later in the same year as he had attended the Society meeting, Adey submitted papers to the Society for Psychical Research, which were considered important enough to be summarised in C D Broad's *Lectures on Psychical Research* in 1962.[14] These are case studies of psychical apparitions, one of which is prefaced with the following:

> The accounts of the following case were collected by Mr More Adey of Wotton-under-Edge, who had seen the persons concerned. The written documents are undated, but appear to have been sent to him in the latter part of 1883.

On 29 January 1880 Adey was admitted to Lincoln's Inn, but although he called himself a barrister in census returns and is noted as such on his death certificate he was never called to the Bar. His dues continued to be paid until 1927 but Lincoln's Inn has no record of activity beyond the financial.

The 1881 census records Adey living as a lodger in the house of George and Mary Powell in Raphael Street, close now to Knightsbridge tube station. His occupation is given as "student, Oxford and Lincoln's Inn". Although there is no evidence that Adey pursued young men in the same way as some of his friends, it is worth noting that he was living very near to the Knightsbridge roller-skating rink which was a favoured pick-up spot, including for Lord Alfred Douglas.

Notes

1 'Training in Simple and Religious Habits': Keble and its First Warden, by Geoffrey Rowell in *The History of the University of Oxford Vol VII, Nineteenth Century Oxford, Part 2,* edited by M G Brock and M C Curtis, p. 178

2 *The Street of Wonderful Possibilities: Whistler, Wilde and Sargent in Tite Street,* Devon Cox, Frances Lincoln 2015, p. 39 et seq

3 *In Victorian Days,* Sir David Hunter Blair, Longmans, Green 1939, p. 89

4 Rowell, p. 179

5 *The Medieval Manuscripts of Keble College,* Oxford, M B Parkes, 1979, p. xi

6 *The Complete Letters of Oscar Wilde,* edited by Merlin Holland and Rupert Hart-Davis, Fourth Estate 2000, p. 1179

7 *Oxford Characters,* Will Rothenstein, John Lane 1896

8 Hunter Blair, p. 78

9 Rules of the Oxford University Catholic Club, Rule 10

10 *Complete Letters,* p. 39. Wilde says this in a letter to A C Ward in [March] 1877

11 Quoted in *Gerard Manley Hopkins: A Very Private Life,* Robert Bernard Martin, Harper Collins 1991, p. 292

12 *Ibid*

13 *Complete Letters,* p. 38

14 *Lectures on Psychical Research,* by C D Broad, Routledge and Kegan Paul, 1962, p. 142

3. THE WILDE CIRCLE

The years between 1881 and 1890 form another of the blank periods in Adey's life. There are suggestions in later correspondence that he may have travelled in Europe and, perhaps, in Scandinavia. After 1890 he was often said to be abroad and he is unlikely only to have started travelling then. If nothing else happened during those years, he met Robert Ross, a meeting which was to have a profound effect on the rest of his life. How that meeting occurred is a mystery, but it is possible to see connections from Frank Costelloe in Oxford to Count Stenbock and thus to Ross. It is then almost certain that Robert Ross introduced Adey to Wilde. Ross and Adey were thought of by many as a couple by the beginning of 1892 and probably by 1890; this seems to have been less a romantic couple as a pair of constant companions who worked well together. This was not an unusual arrangement; as J G P Delaney says of Ricketts and Shannon:

> What seems very obvious to us was not so to their contemporaries. Their generation was much less 'knowing' than ours. Many men remained bachelors, or shared a house for company and convenience, without any of the raised eyebrows or speculation that have become common since the popularization of psychological theories.[1]

While Ricketts and Shannon lived together for many years, and while Ricketts's true nature was homosexual, he was not able to admit it for many years and probably then first to Ross; he is unlikely to have touched on the subject with Wilde and, again his biographer says:

> After a quarrel [with Shannon] Ricketts noted that he was 'grateful that we do not see each other as others see us': this seems to mean that they regarded themselves more as individuals sharing common interests than as the unit others considered them to be; they were two celibates sharing an ideal, as William Rothenstein's phrase for them – 'the sisters of the Vale' – suggests.[2]

Adey was certainly accepting of homosexual activity; Douglas's letters to him are often explicit about Douglas's and Ross's relationships with young men, but there is no evidence that Adey took an active part. Adey and Ross may have often shared an address, but they spent a great deal of time apart and it is evident from the correspondence during Wilde's imprisonment that they did not co-ordinate their lives well.

Emma Elizabeth, Adey's youngest sister, married in the parish church of Wotton under Edge in June 1886. Her husband was the splendidly named Ponsonby Augustus Moore Sullivan, the son of the Rev. James Sullivan. Ponsonby had been born in Australia, but his father's most recent living had been in county Limerick in Ireland. The inclusion of Moore in Ponsonby's name suggests there may have been a family connection, but the probable route to his connection with the Adeys is that he went up to Keble College in 1877, while Adey was still there. Ponsonby shared Adey's antiquarian interests, and many years later published a paper on 'Scratch Dials in Gloucestershire'.[3]

Shortly after the marriage, Sullivan was appointed curate of St Oswald's, Durham, and both Ross and Adey were to spend time there. He almost certainly met Wilde, and there are presentation copies of books from Ross and Wilde to Sullivan. It is unlikely, however, that, as one bookseller has suggested, Sullivan and Wilde were lovers.

In 1890 Adey had edited a volume of Balzac's short stories with the extraordinary Count Stenbock.[4] Of the eleven stories in the volume, Stenbock had translated two and Adey, under the pseudonym of William Wilson, the rest. It is clear that Adey also provided the "Prefatory Notice" which includes a wonderful prefiguring of Lady Bracknell:

> Translations from Balzac are met by the objection that people who are cultivated enough to understand them will probably have learnt French at school, and can read them in the original language. But there are many people of education and mental power who cannot read any foreign language with pleasure. Moreover, the excellent system of our schools, where some of the best years of life are spent in acquiring a distaste for all education, is sufficient to ensure ignorance of any subject on the curriculum.

It is not clear how Adey's own knowledge of foreign languages developed, but he apparently travelled extensively in Europe and went on to publish translations from German and Norwegian.

The book was published by the firm of Walter Scott (no connection to the author of *Waverley*) which had, at the end of 1889 published Frederick Wedmore's biography of Balzac in their Great Writers Series. For the bibliographer the various Walter Scott series pose a number of problems, the principal one being that they rarely carry a date. Stenbock and Adey's Balzac was part of the Camelot Series which, as Camelot Classics, first appeared in 1885 and eventually ran to 131 titles. In 1887 Camelot

Classics became the Camelot Series and in 1892 became the Scott Library. They appear in different bindings but they were well produced and cheap; the prospectus described "a comprehensive Prose Library" which would be "cheap, without the reproach which cheapness usually implies" and would provide a "complete Prose Library for the People".[5] The series editor for the first several years was Ernest Rhys, who was later the founding editor of the Everyman Library.

Rhys claims to have met Stenbock at the Chelsea home of the poet William Bell Scott in 1886 or 1887. Rhys's memoirs are not always reliable, but he describes Stenbock at that first meeting as unusual: "very fair hair beautifully curled, and a blond, round blue-eyed face, with yellow eyebrows"; "like a magnified child".[6] He does not mention meeting Adey and we must assume that the commission for the Balzac stories was given to Stenbock, even though he eventually made a much smaller contribution than the always self-effacing Adey.

Adey had known Stenbock for some years by the time the Balzac translation came out. Stenbock had gone up to Balliol College, Oxford in 1879, the year Adey converted to Catholicism, but stayed only four terms. By 1882 Adey and Stenbock were such close friends that, on the journey home from the family estates in Estonia, Stenbock wrote to a friend in London seeking urgent news of Adey because Stenbock was haunted by the idea that Adey was dead.[7] The likelihood must be that Stenbock, who had been raised a Catholic, was instrumental in Adey's religious conversion.

Stenbock was also a close friend and patron of Simeon Solomon and we know that Adey owned several drawings by Solomon (as did Ross and Wilde). An exhibition of Jewish Art and Antiquities at the Whitechapel Art Gallery in 1906 featured fifty six works by Simeon Solomon of which nine were lent by Adey, four by Ross and three by the Carfax Gallery. Here we may see the kernel of what Stephen Calloway describes as the Cenacle.[8] This is a useful term, but it is one that was often applied to literary groups in France and Britain and there is no evidence to suggest that this particular group so designated themselves; it may have been applied later. The word cenacle means an upper room, in particular the one in which the biblical Last Supper took place, and, unlike the Rhymers' Club and other groups of the time, Ross, Adey and friends do not seem to have favoured any particular meeting place outside of their own homes.

At the end of 1891 Adey published – again as William Wilson – the first English translation of Ibsen's verse drama *Brand*.[9] William Archer had already published translations of the prose dramas, and Montgomery Hyde suggested that Adey worked with Archer on early Ibsen productions.[10] Adey translated the Norwegian verse into English prose. His preface justifies this decision by citing "the highest examples":

> It is only necessary to mention Dr Carlyle's translation of the *Inferno*, Dr Butcher and Mr Lang's translation of the *Odyssey*, Monsieur Stéphane Mallarmé's translation of Poe's poems into French, and Matthew Arnold's exquisite version of the Fifteenth Idyll of Theokritus, as the most successful translations of verse with which I am acquainted. On the other hand, Shelley's fragment from *El Magico Prodigioso* is his own exquisite verse, but it is not a faithful reproduction of Calderon; the greater poet eclipses the lesser. Mr Florence McCarthy, as a verse translator of the great Spanish dramatist, gives no truer idea of the original than Pope or Mr William Morris of Homer, or Carey or Longfellow of Dante, or Conington of Vergil or Horace. The work of these poets no doubt shows ingenuity and scholarship, and, in some instances, poetical taste; but it gives little idea of the power and charm of the originals, and frequently wholly obscures their meaning. Indeed the greater the poet who translates, the greater is the barrier which his personality raises between the reader and the author.
>
> How far the present version falls short of so high a standard I am painfully conscious, but at least I owe no apology for writing it in prose.

The critics by and large did not comment on Adey's translation, although the *Bristol Mercury* welcomed it – not because of the translation itself, of which it rather dismissively said:

> The translation appears to be satisfactory; it is certainly good idiomatic English prose.

The paper's welcome was more about what the translation did not do:

> The Norwegian dramatist Henrik Ibsen has been very much talked about in England during the last year or two, to a large extent by a number of flies on the wheel, nonentities who hope to make themselves important by hanging to the skirts of a great man's literary garments. Mr Wilson is not one of these, for he dissents from an Ibsen cult altogether, and objects to reading into a man's writings meanings which he never intended. In the translation of "Brand" he has, therefore, left out any notes, even in explanation of national customs, because he thinks that Ibsen should become directly known before he is made the subject of

> critical analysis. This is quite right, only it would not serve the purpose of those who have Ibsenism in hand.[11]

Other reviewers' problems were with Ibsen rather than the translation. The *Birmingham Daily Post* began its review (a relatively long one) combatively:

> We find considerable difficulty in speaking of this production. If our task were simply to say whether or not we like it and to assign some reason for our judgment, it would be comparatively easy. But whether we like it or not "Brand" is a work of art, and in judging of a work of art one should note the author's aim and measure what degree of success has attended his efforts to attain it. Here at the outset we are puzzled. The world to which Ibsen introduces us is so strange that we find it more difficult to realise it than the scenery and characters of the Arabian Nights. Every line of the play seems to indicate some terribly earnest moral purpose, but what that purpose is we have not the foggiest idea.[12]

The book was probably the most commercially successful of Adey's publications, going through several editions and staying in print for many years. It was not until 1912, however, that it reached the stage. On 10 and 11 November, "The Playactors" – a "useful society" who had "introduced to our stage a number of native and foreign plays which the average manager would consider outside the pale of theatrical enterprise" – performed it at the Court Theatre.

Reviews were scarce and the critic for the *Yorkshire Post* summed up why:

> If one of the aims of the Playactors be to act the unactable, it may be said to have been consummated at the Court Theatre yesterday afternoon when Ibsen's "Brand" was presented to a calm, impassive audience which included Mr Bernard Shaw.[13]

It was an ambitious production with thirty-one named actors, although if the stage directions in the book were followed not all of these would have appeared on stage. Not least among the production's problems was the staging of the "final avalanche, which buries Brand and fills the whole valley". The Court's resources were not up to such spectacular effects.

On 14 February 1892, at the first night of *Lady Windermere's Fan,* Adey is noted in Wilde's company for the first time. Wilde was accompanied by a group of young men (although Adey was nearly 34 by this time) including Ross, Reggie Turner, Edward Shelley, Pierre Louys and Graham

Robertson.[14] Whether Adey sported one of the green carnations Oscar had instructed them to wear, history does not record. Graham Robertson told the story in his autobiography of being asked to wear the carnation:

> "Go to Such-and-such a shop and order a green carnation buttonhole for to-morrow night. No, I know there's no such thing, but they arrange them somehow at that shop; dye them, I suppose. I want a good many men to wear them to-morrow – it will annoy the public."
>
> "But why annoy the public?"
>
> "It likes to be annoyed. A young man on the stage will wear a green carnation; people will stare at it and wonder. Then they will look round the house and see every here and there more and more little specks of mystic green. 'This must be some secret symbol,' they will say. 'What on earth can it mean?'"
>
> "And what does it mean?" I asked.
>
> "Nothing whatever," said Oscar, "but that is just what nobody will guess."[15]

Nothing else in Adey's life suggests that he wanted to "annoy the public". Turner was obviously close to both Ross and Adey at this time; Douglas says that Turner shared rooms with them in Kensington for a while.

Earlier the same day, the critic and expert on church architecture, Aymer Vallance had hosted a small reception in his rooms in Wells Street, off Mortimer Street. Here he presented his new discovery, Aubrey Beardsley, to some of his "most intimate friends", including Ross and Adey. Vallance was a recent convert to Catholicism, having been an Anglican curate. He had heard of Beardsley from a fellow clergyman and had asked to see his portfolio only in January 1892, but wasted no time in presenting his art to his friends. Adey, translator of Balzac, was apparently astonished by Beardsley's knowledge of the French writer and Ross was equally impressed. But, as Beardsley's biographer says:

> He outflanked his literary and artistic listeners by introducing the subject of music, only to draw back, seemingly 'disappointed' that none of the company shared his passion.[16]

Ross made no secret of his lack of musical interest; in his contribution to *Roads to Rome: Being Personal Records of Some of the More Recent Converts to the Catholic Faith* in 1901 he says, "I dislike music now, both in and out of church, and I would prefer all instruments banished from it".[17] Adey's published work and extant letters show no interest in music. However, the only book from his library I have been able to examine is Edmonstoune

Duncan's *The Story of Minstrelsy*, which Adey has extensively and carefully annotated, although the nature of the annotations suggests that this may demonstrate his interest in history rather than in music.

Ross of course took Beardsley up immediately and was later to write the first book on Beardsley (with an iconography by Vallance).[18] Adey became an early collector, favouring pictures with a Renaissance feeling, but also appreciating grotesques. His purchases included "The Litany of Mary Magdalen", which had been one of the pictures Beardsley showed to Edward Burne Jones in July 1891, and the slightly later "Incipit Vita Nova". Both these pictures are now in America. He also owned Beardsley's head of Francesca di Rimini.[19]

In October 1904 the Carfax Gallery, under the direction of Ross and Adey, put on the first comprehensive exhibition of Beardsley's art. Roger Fry gave the exhibition a very positive review in the *Athenaeum*.[20] By the time Ross published his book, *Aubrey Beardsley*, in 1909 "The Litany of Mary Magdalen" is listed as "Formerly Property of More Adey, Esq" and "Incipit Vita Nova" is listed as "Property of Messrs Carfax & Co".

Writers on Beardsley have suggested that the title of Beardsley's novel, *Under the Hill*, contained both an erotic reference and a nod to Adey's house in Wotton. I see no reason for the latter to be true. There is no evidence that Beardsley ever visited Wotton and the first chapter of the book ends with Tannhäuser stepping "into the shadowy corridor that ran into the bosom of the wan hill". There is no reason why that should refer to a house in Gloucestershire, and there is nothing about the gentle slope on which Adey's house sits to suggest erotic adventures.

James G Nelson, in his book on Leonard Smithers says that Adey was a shareholder in Smithers's publishing business, but the evidence for that has not resurfaced.[21] If true, it might explain an acquaintance with Beardsley beyond the original meeting.

In the same year as they met Beardsley - 1892 - Ross and Adey collaborated on a new edition of *Melmoth the Wanderer*, jointly writing a long introduction for the publishers Richard Bentley.[22] The editors were anonymous, although they added a preface – dated February 1892 – in which they asked "to record their best thanks to Mr Oscar Wilde and Lady Wilde (Speranza) for several details with regard to Maturin's life". Charles Robert Maturin, the author of *Melmoth the Wanderer* was Wilde's great uncle and the book was important to Wilde. When he was to be released from prison in 1897, Ross suggested Melmoth as a pseudonym;

he adopted this and the first name Sebastian after a favoured saint. This is the only known explicitly collaborative effort, although the pseudonym, William Wilson, which is usually said to be Adey's seems to have been a joint one. Ross signed a presentation inscription as William Wilson at least once, as did Adey as can be seen from an inscription in Adey's translation of Bjornsen's *Pastor Sang* from 1893. It might be assumed, given Adey's interest in the supernatural that the name William Wilson was taken from the story of the same name by Edgar Allan Poe, which is about a man and his double – Ross and Adey. Poe was an interest of Beardsley's as well, and Poe's raven may have been the inspiration for Adey's adoption of a pet bird after Ross's death.

William Wilson published another translation in 1892 – of Maurice Maeterlinck's *The Intruder*. However, this brings its own little mystery for a prefatory "Note" says:

> The following translation of *L'Intruse* is based upon a rough sketch of a translation by Mr William Wilson, to whom the author had originally given the permission to translate the work, and who, at the moment when it had to appear, was through absence from England prevented from completing and revising his version.

Where he was and for how long is not known, but Adey's letters often claim illness or absence abroad as excuses for not responding to correspondence.

Pastor Sang, in 1893, had a cover design by Aymer Vallance and a frontispiece by Beardsley. The William Wilson identity was kept a close secret; as late as August 1896 Arthur Clifton wrote to Adey that "Really I never knew you were William Wilson whom I have often heard of".

No more publications by Adey or "William Wilson" have been traced, although in 1899 Wilde wrote to Adey saying, "I am much interested to hear of your book on Dante".[23] Even this sounds as if it may have been a collaboration with Ross; Wilde continued, "Robbie, with ostentatious modesty, has told me nothing about his story at all".

The first evidence of another link in the web of '90s relationships came in June 1893 when a contribution by Count Stenbock appeared in the Oxford undergraduate magazine *The Spirit Lamp*, then edited by Lord Alfred Douglas. This was "The Other Side: A Breton Legend" and appeared in the same issue as "The Disciple" by Oscar Wilde. Stenbock's name is misspelled at the end of the story and in the list of contents on the cover of the magazine.

Adey already knew Douglas; indeed, he may have known him before Douglas met Wilde. It was Douglas's cousin, the poet Lionel Johnson, who introduced Wilde and Douglas in 1890 and there is a poem called "July" in Johnson's collection *Ireland and Other Poems* which is dated 1889 and dedicated to More Adey. If Johnson and Adey were that close by 1889 it is probable that Douglas would have been introduced to Adey. The familiarity between Wilde, Douglas and Adey is clear in the first written communication between Wilde and Adey, which appeared in November of 1893 – a telegram:

> Bosie has influenza and is very pale. The wicked Lane has been routed with slaughter. I have begun a mystery play[24]

This was sent from St James's Street and signed Oscar. The familiarity rather undermines Robert Ross's recollections as expressed in a letter to Douglas in June 1897:

> Before the Queensberry trouble, More was not a friend of Oscar's at all. I do not think he ever liked O particularly. He certainly disapproved of him very much, and I don't think he had read any of Oscar's works. He was, however, very fond of you & admired you very much. Directly O was in low water, he became as fond of O I believe as any friend of O's could be, because that is More's nature. ... He gave £200 to Humphreys for O's defence.[25]

As will become clear, the relationship between Ross and Douglas by this time was precarious, and it may have been that Ross was in some way trying to protect Adey from guilt by association. However, it may be that Ross was correct and that Adey – who is notably absent from stories of Wilde before the trials and with whom there appears to have been no correspondence beyond the one telegram – was only part of a group around Wilde because of his association with Ross.

By November 1893 Adey had been involved in an episode which prefigured his role in the Wilde trials two years later. Biscoe Wortham, head of a school in Bruges, discovered through an indiscreet letter written by Douglas, that one of his pupils had been seduced by Ross. Suspicion aroused, he questioned his own sons and found that Philip Wortham had been seduced three times by Ross. There were threats of legal action by the father of the first boy and vague threats of some sort of action by Biscoe Wortham, who by this time had implicated both Douglas and Wilde as well as Ross, describing him as "one of a gang of the most brutal ruffians who spend their time in seducing and prostituting boys".[26] Ross tried to negotiate but was not successful and involved his solicitor, Sir George Lewis. Finally the negotiations were taken over by Adey, who was able to report that no legal action would be taken. Whether there was any other form of compensation is not known.

Adey had been the soul of discretion. Ross – partly for health reasons and partly to distance him from his companions – was sent to Davos by his parents and put in the charge of his brother Jack. He wrote to Douglas from there:

> I am not allowed to live in London for two years. As the purse strings are in their hands and a stoppage is threatened, I have to submit. A[dey] had concealed everything, but the worthy Rev. Mr Squeers [Wortham] wrote a full and particular account of how things were to my brother. It was news to him, as A[dey] had hitherto concealed everything but the trouble with the noisy military gentleman.[27]

This episode seems to define Adey: working quietly in the background, not divulging anything of himself, trusted by his friends and always self-effacing. He carried on this way during Wilde's trials and imprisonment, but this very self- possession and resulting trust led to much less satisfactory outcomes.

The only extensive correspondence extant with Adey is a series of letters from Douglas between 1895 and 1900.[28] Adey's side of the exchange is missing so many of the references are without context and mysterious, but they provide something of a commentary on events during the period.

Notes

1 *Charles Ricketts, A Biography*, J G P Delaney, Oxford University Press 1990, p. 25

2 Delaney, p. 24

3 "Scratch Dials in Gloucestershire", Rev. Ponsonby Sullivan, in *Transactions* of the Bristol and Gloucestershire Archaeological Society, Vol. 26, 1924

4 *Shorter Stories from Balzac: English Versions by William Wilson and the Count Stenbock: With a Prefatory Notice*, The Walter Scott Publishing Co, 1890. In early September 1890 Walter Scott had advertised the book as Balzac, Honoré de, "Don Juan; or The Elixir of a Long Life, and other stories". No translators were named and it was announced as having paper covers.

5 *The Walter Scott Publishing Co Ltd: A Forgotten Northeastern Publisher*, John R Turner, History of the Book Trade in the North, PH60 February 1993

6 *Wales England Wed,* Ernest Rhys, Dent 1940, p. 76

7 *Stenbock, Yeats and the Nineties,* John Adlard, Cecil & Amelia Woolf, 1969 p. 23. This remains the best and most comprehensive account of Stenbock's life.

8 *Aubrey Beardsley,* Stephen Calloway, V&A Publications, 1998, p. 64

9 *Brand, A Dramatic Poem* by Henrik Ibsen, translated by William Wilson, Methuen 1891

10 *Oscar Wilde: The Aftermath,* H Montgomery Hyde, Methuen 1963, p. 44n

11 *Bristol Mercury* 16 April 1892

12 *Birmingham Daily Post* 16 December 1912

13 *Yorkshire Post* 12 November 1912

14 *Oscar Wilde,* Richard Ellmann, Hamish Hamilton 1987, p. 344

15 *Time Was,* W Graham Robertson, Hamish Hamilton 1931 p. 135

16 *Aubrey Beardsley, a Biography,* Matthew Sturgis, Harper Collins 1998, p. 95

17 *Roads to Rome: Being Personal Records of Some of the More Recent Converts to the Catholic Faith,* edited by J G Raupert, Longmans 1901, p. 234

18 *Aubrey Beardsley,* Robert Ross, John Lane The Bodley Head 1909

19 *Aubrey Beardsley: A Catalogue Raisonné,* Linda Gertner Zatlin, Yale University Press 2016, Catalogue numbers 184, 198, 243

20 *Athenaeum* review reprinted in *Vision and Design,* Roger Fry, Penguin 1937

21 *Publisher to the Decadents: Leonard Smithers in the Careers of Beardsley, Wilde, Dowson,* James G Nelson, Rivendale Press, 2000, p. 95

22 *Melmoth the Wanderer,* Charles Robert Maturin, Richard Bentley 1892. The work, in three volumes, bears the imprint of Richard Bentley on the title pages but Macmillan appears on the spines.

23 *The Complete Letters of Oscar Wilde,* edited by Merlin Holland and Rupert Hart-Davis, Fourth Estate 2000, p. 1129

24 Holland and Hart-Davis, p. 577

25 Ross to Douglas 23 June 1897, William Andrews Clark Library

26 Quoted in *Wilde's Devoted Friend: a Life of Robert Ross 1869-1918,* Maureen Borland, Lennard Publishing 1990, p. 34

27 Quoted in Borland, p. 35

28 I consulted this series at Magdalen College, where the texts are prefaced by a note by H Montgomery Hyde: "The following letters are taken from a transcript formerly in the possession of A J A Symons Esq". P204/3/7C/1

4. WILDE IN PRISON

Following the November 1893 telegram there was no further explicit relationship with Wilde until a letter from Holloway prison on 9 April 1895, after which the correspondence floodgates opened. That letter, addressed jointly to Ross and Adey but clearly delivered to Adey, asked them to pass on thanks to well-wishers and to inform the committees of the New Travellers Club and the Albemarle Club that Wilde wished to resign his memberships.[1] It is obvious from this letter – one of two which Wilde wrote that day, the other to the Leversons – that he had already identified Ross and Adey as two people who should take care of his affairs while he was out of the world. A third was to be Arthur Bellamy Clifton who was effectively already Wilde's solicitor. Still only thirty-two, Clifton is another man whose entry into the Wilde circle of friends is unclear. He may have met Wilde at Oxford because, although he went to Cambridge, his father was Professor of Experimental Philosophy at Oxford. He would not have met Ross at Cambridge as he had left before Ross arrived and had been at a different college. While he may have experimented in his youth, Clifton does not seem to have been a part of any homosexual coterie; indeed all Wilde's friends appear to have got on very well with his wife during this period.

The William Andrews Clark Library holds a great deal of the correspondence of this period, some of it in the shape of the meticulous copies and drafts which Adey made of his own letters; indeed, it is often unclear whether letters were actually sent, at least in the form drafted. A high proportion of the Clark's Adey holdings consists of scraps of unrelated information, lists of names, to-do lists, and lists of questions which Adey felt he needed to ask about Wilde's affairs. He was the focal point for letters from Wilde, Douglas, various legal firms representing Wilde and Constance, the Queensberry family and others.

Wilde was arrested in Lord Alfred Douglas's room at the Cadogan Hotel, Sloane Street, in the early evening of 5 April 1895 and taken to Bow Street. Ross was at the hotel with him but there was no sign of Adey. He had not been involved in giving advice for the libel trial against Queensberry, and the first sign of him during the whole process was at Wilde's first criminal trial when, according to Compton Mackenzie, Adey and Stewart Headlam accompanied Wilde to the Old Bailey "for the second trial" (presumably the first criminal trial). Mackenzie described Adey as "the vaguest man I ever met" and believed that turning up for court must have taken "a miracle of concentration". Mackenzie's recollections, however, cannot always be trusted; he states that it was Ross, rather than Adey, and Headlam who met Wilde on his release from prison.[2]

Local historians of Wotton-under-Edge have suggested that Adey persuaded his own mother to put up the money for Wilde's defence. Though there is no evidence for this beyond Ross's letter to Douglas of June 1897 quoted in the previous chapter, it is unlikely that Adey had £200 of his own to use and his mother is the obvious source. There are other indications of Adey's early involvement in the legal process. Richard Ellmann suggests a convoluted process for raising Wilde's bail whereby Ernest Leverson may have approached Selwyn Image who in turn approached Stewart Headlam.[3] Image had been a founding member with Headlam of the Anti-Puritan League and lived only a few doors from him. On Headlam's death in 1924 Image said that Headlam and Arthur Mackmurdo were the oldest of all his close friends. According to Headlam's biographer, Image said that

> the party who solicited his good offices was a member of a City business firm who was disbarred by the articles of partnership from going bail for anybody, and adds that he himself was in no position to furnish the money. That was why he appealed to Stewart Headlam[4]

According to Douglas's brother, Leverson made up the final £700 of the surety, but there is no reason to believe that Leverson knew Image or would approach him directly on so delicate a matter. One man who knew all the parties involved was Adey; he knew Image and had certainly corresponded with and met Headlam; we know also that Wilde had met Headlam twice before the trials and I suspect that it was Adey who introduced them, although Grant Richards includes Headlam in his list of habitués of the Crown public house in Charing Cross Road along with Wilde.[5] It was to be Adey and Headlam who together met Wilde on his release from Pentonville in 1897.

Stewart Headlam was no stranger to the worlds which Wilde inhabited: his artistic credentials had long been established, not only by being a founder of the Church and Stage Guild in 1879 with its mission to break down the "prejudice against theatres, actors, music hall artists, stage singers, and dancers", but by his commissioning of furniture for his Bloomsbury home from the Century Guild (furniture important enough to be illustrated in *The Building News*). Selwyn Image said that his "love of refined surroundings was genuine and deep", and when the Leversons visited Headlam's home on the morning of Wilde's release from Pentonville, Ada gave this picture of the drawing-room, it

> was full of Burne-Jones and Rossetti pictures, Morris wallpaper and curtains, in fact an example of the decoration of the early 'eighties, very beautiful in its way, and very like the aesthetic rooms Oscar had once loved.[6]

The homosexual element of Wilde's life would probably not have shocked Headlam either. As his biographer says, "If Headlam ever despaired of his priestly vocation, it was in the winter of 1878-79. He had no prospect of employment, his bishop did not trust him, and he had discovered that his wife was a lesbian".[7] Headlam attributed the broadening of his mind to his favourite master at Eton, William Johnson Cory, author (anonymously) of the collection of Uranian verse, *Ionica*. Fortunately for both Headlam and Wilde, a private income meant that his unemployability was not a great stumbling block, although he had been elected to the London School Board in 1882 and it is in that role that it seems Adey first made his acquaintance.

To add to Adey's woes, on 26 April, the day the first criminal trial opened, his old friend Stenbock died. In his will – of which Adey was joint executor with Frank Costelloe – he left to Adey his opal ring and all his jewellery, silver and other effects (less two silver dishes to be returned to Estonia), expressing the hope that he would distribute some among other friends, especially Ross. He also left him all papers, manuscripts and literary remains, with a particular wish that they should be published, "but I leave the publication or not to him as in his own uncontrolled discretion he may think fit".[8] Adey never did publish them, although in the 1920s he was clearly having discussions with Christopher Millard about publishing a Collected Works and offering Stenbock "remainders". In a letter to A J A Symons in May 1925 he said that his Stenbock manuscripts were packed up waiting to hear from Arthur Symons and Ernest Rhys who were proposing publication. Nothing was to come of this proposal.

Ernest Rhys, Adey's first editor, had seen Stenbock fairly recently and described how "he had changed from the boyish Stenbock I first knew! His curly locks were gone, his lips bloodless, and there was no sparkle now in his china-blue eyes." After that last meeting the "news of his death came through his friend Adey, who had collaborated with him in his Balzac book. He left me a bequest of some of his favourite books, Rosicrucian and romantic, with his fantastic serpentine bookmark".[9] This is the only mention of Adey in Rhys's memoirs and the reference to collaboration sounds less than fulsome when Adey had contributed more than eighty percent of the work.

In August J G Muddiman, solicitor, placed an advertisement in the *Morning Post* requiring that:

> all Creditors and other Persons Claiming Debts or Liabilities affecting the estate of Eric Magnus Andreas Harry Stanislaus Stenbock Count Stenbock, of Kolk Konda, Kida and Neuenhoff in the Province of Esthonia, in the Empire of Russia, and of 21 Gloucester-walk, Camden-hill, Kensington, in the County of Middlesex, deceased (who died on the 26th day of April, 1895, at Withdeane Hall, Patcham, Brighton, in the County of Sussex, and whose will was proved in the Principal Registry of the Probate Division of Her Majesty's High Court of Justice on the 21st day of June, 1895 by More Adey of Wooton-under-Edge, in the County of Gloucester, Esquire, and Benjamin Francis Conn Costelloe of 33 Chancery-lane, in the County of Middlesex, barrister-at-law, the Executors therein named) are hereby required to Send Particulars in writing of their respective Claims and Demands to the undersigned on or before the 20th day of September next, at the expiration of such time the said Executors will proceed to distribute the Assets of the said Testator amongst the parties entitled thereto.[10]

Until Adey mentions Stenbock's manuscripts in letters to Christopher Millard many years later, we hear no more of Stenbock or Costelloe.

Constance Wilde had certainly known Ross since 1887, when he stayed with the Wildes for three months at Tite Street and in 1895, as Franny Moyle says, "Constance seems to have become reliant on Robbie's preparedness to play messenger between his two friends Constance and Oscar".[11] Despite the closeness of Ross and Adey, it would seem that Constance did not know Adey when the trials began. A letter to him signed C M Holland from Heidelberg in August 1896 begins "Dear Mr Rady", as if she had only heard his name in conversation.[12]

He seems to have been equally unknown to the rest of the family. Lily Wilde, Willie Wilde's wife, wrote to Adey in October 1895 as "Mr Moor Adye", although they had met when he had given her news of Wilde in prison. She recounts after a visit to Wilde that "he seemed gratified when I told him how you had kindly come up to give me news of him". At the time of Lady Wilde's death in February of the following year, Willie Wilde wrote to Adey, clearly knowing him reasonably well by that time. He thanked him "& all good friends of Oscar's for the token of sympathy with her in my sorrow" and hoped that Adey would be able to call the following day to "decide what is best in poor Oscar's interest". Surprisingly he added "I don't know Mr Ross but you can thank him from me for his sympathy". It is obvious that Wilde had been keeping family life separate from his other interests.[13] A letter from Wilde in 1900 praised Adey for his attention to Lady Wilde when she was ill; perhaps Willie did not know of this.

Constance did, however, know Arthur Clifton and appears to have liked him. Clifton and his new wife had visited the Wildes while they were holidaying in Felbrigg, Norfolk in 1892, and Clifton had shared a box with Constance at the first night of *Lady Windermere's Fan*, while Adey was with Wilde's more intimate friends elsewhere in the theatre. As Wilde's solicitor, Clifton was joint trustee, with Carlos Blacker, of the Wildes' marriage settlement.

Clifton, Adey and Ross – unlikely as it may seem – appear also to have shared a fondness for cycling. Clifton wrote to Adey in Wotton in September 1896 saying that "When you return we must make expeditions" and suggesting that Adey should "tell Oscar of the bicycling rage".

In the very early days of Wilde's imprisonment, Adey was called on to steer a careful course in judging the public presentation of Wilde's case. An English Quaker and aspiring poet from Newcastle called James H Wilson had visited Douglas in Rouen in May and, impressed by Douglas's claims about the judicial system, determined to publish a defence of Wilde. This was to be called *Some Gentle Criticisms of British Justice*, and he felt it important to get Adey's approval for the project. Adey's name was not widely known as an associate of Wilde, so it is fair to assume that Douglas had put him forward to Wilson.

Adey proved elusive, but wrote to Wilson to say that he was "equally the friend of Mr Wilde and Lord Alfred Douglas, but this is not the case with many people who are anxious to help Mr Oscar Wilde". He felt it necessary to emphasise Wilde's "excellent understanding" with his wife, rather than his "romantic friendship" with Douglas. For himself, Adey claimed that as one of Wilde's friends his public attitude should be one of "cold reserve and indifference". The pamphlet Wilson intended does not appear ever to have been distributed although his persistence did result in various pieces sympathetic to Wilde appearing in *Reynolds' Newspaper*.[14]

The attempted management of Wilde's financial affairs by Ross and Adey during and after Wilde's imprisonment, and Wilde's reactions to their lack of success, mark a low point in the relationship between Wilde and Adey. But there is little evidence of much happening on this front until

Wilde's letter to Ross on 10 March 1896 in which his life interest in the marriage settlement was mentioned for the first time.

In this letter Wilde passed on his thanks to Adey "for exerting himself for books" and said "Ask him to express also my gratitude to the lady who lives at Wimbledon". This latter was in response to Adela Schuster's gift of £1000 to Wilde when he was out on bail. He had passed it to Ernest Leverson for safekeeping; an act which was to lead to much acrimony the following year. Adey had arranged with the Home Office for Wilde to be provided with more books.

The ins and outs of these financial wranglings have been covered well elsewhere – most recently in J Robert Maguire's book on Carlos Blacker.[15] But, in the light of Wilde's subsequent complaints, it is worth remembering that it was Adey who tried to raise funds for Wilde, who organised the books to be delivered to him in prison, who drafted the petition to the Home Secretary to commute Wilde's sentence, who communicated with the prison about the arrangements for Wilde's release, who met Wilde at the prison gates and who accompanied him to Dieppe. Demonstrating again his punctiliousness is the receipt for £25 written out by Adey on 19 May 1897 and signed by Wilde with the subscription "with deep and sincere thanks". Much of this activity may have been ill thought out, but it was certainly well intentioned.

Despite describing himself as a barrister, and being the son of a solicitor, Adey had no legal training. Ross had even less understanding of the law. Arthur Clifton, nominally Wilde's solicitor, was not conversant with the law on divorce (although he was to gain personal experience of it a few years later), and the legal firms employed by Ross and Adey seem not to have been specialists in that area.

The postponed bankruptcy hearing had taken place on 12 November 1895 and Wilde was moved to Reading gaol on 21 November, where Adey was probably his first visitor, on the 30th. There was presumably some discussion of "business" during this visit. Douglas had written asking Adey to intercede with Wilde, although his letter did not arrive until after the visit. Adey wrote to him sympathetically, but urged Douglas to "try to show the love which I know you have for him, by the most difficult of all ways – waiting". He indicated that Wilde and Constance ought to be together for a while after Wilde's release, but that such a reconciliation – with "a woman with a torn heart" – could not last. The remainder of this letter is lost, so we cannot say what his justification for this view might have been or whether it was based on his talk with Wilde.

Adey did not visit Wilde in prison again until June 1896; Ross and Sherard had visited the previous month, after which Wilde, in writing to Ross, had said, "Kind regards to More, whom I would so like to see".

Adey's time between Wilde's trials and now had to a great extent been taken up with placating Douglas. They had been in constant communication and their relations seem to have continued to be relatively cordial. Sybil Queensberry had asked Douglas's cousin, Lionel Johnson, to visit him in Rouen but Johnson was not available so she asked Fr Sebastian Bowden, the fashionable priest at the Brompton Oratory in Kensington to find "some steady and trustworthy friend to look after her son Ld A" and Adey agreed in early June to do so when he felt, as Bowden put it, "secure as regards R who certainly has the prior claim on your charity". Sybil Queensberry offered to pay his hotel expenses for a month or two "if you manage to stay so long". Bowden clearly knew Adey for he added "I said that I did not think they wd exceed about £3 a week as I know you are a careful man"[16]

Fr Bowden was the priest whom Wilde had visited in 1878, at which meeting Bowden said he "did freely and entirely lay open to me your life's history and your soul's state". Bowden urged Wilde to come and see him again and in "the meantime pray hard and talk little". That last was always going to be difficult for Wilde and instead of visiting he sent Bowden a bunch of lilies. Bowden may also have been the priest who received Adey into the Catholic church in the same year.

Ross went to stay with Douglas later in June and, once he had left for Dieppe, Douglas started pestering Adey to visit, which he did by the end of the month. Douglas was constantly trying to encourage visitors; when Lionel Johnson finally went to see him in Le Havre in the middle of July he wrote to Adey that it "is very important for Bosie's health and peace of mind, that he should be alone as little as possible".[17]

One much desired visitor who seems never to have arrived was the mysterious Charlie Hickey – described by Oscar as "one of the thousand Charlies of London", but, as the son of a retired army major, rather different from many of those other Charlies. Charlie spent time with Bosie in Paris and was then meant to join him in Rouen in June 1895 but had become "a heartless little wretch" for not turning up. Neil McKenna suggests that Charlie had slept with Adey; I personally believe that, while Adey was certainly attracted to men, he was not sexually active, preferring companionship. There are letters from Charlie to Adey in the Clark, mainly about the return of a portmanteau (about which – Charlie assures Adey

– "neither myself or any member of my family have had the bag in use"), but also complaining about Bosie, who had been showering Charlie with telegrams for which Charlie had to pay 12/6, and thanking Adey for all his kindness. Around this time Charlie told Adey that he and his brother were about to take "a new Hotel", which appears to have been the Glen Hotel in Wooda Bay, just outside Lynton in Devon. After his release from prison, Wilde wrote several times to Reggie Turner asking for news of Charlie, and, via Smithers, sent him an inscribed copy of *The Importance of Being Earnest*. At one point in 1897 Wilde bemoaned the fact that Charlie was in America but that visit was probably brief as he is also said to have lived with Turner in the late nineties.

Douglas complained bitterly to Adey about Ross but usually closed his letters with "love to Bobbie". At the end of July 1895 Douglas wrote "I am dull here since you left. .... I must thank you, dear More, for being so kind and nice to me, and am with best love ever yours very affectionately, Bosie". But the next month he complained to his brother that Adey was not responding to his letters and this was followed almost immediately by an unexplained telegram to Adey: "Certainly not. Pomatti exploded long ago. Don't send fanciful telegrams. Why not write?"

Some slight explanation came two days later in a letter where he apologised for a "snappish" telegram and explained "Pomatti turned out a complete fraud, and the subject is a sore one". The name seems to be connected with Wilde's bankruptcy, which Adey appears to have offered to help with, but Douglas urged him not to do anything without consulting his brother Percy, "to prevent useless efforts on your part". The rest of that letter encouraged Adey or Ross to visit him in Sorrento where lodging would cost nothing and board would be only $6^{1/2}$ francs a day.

Ross went to see Douglas at the Villa Caso in Capri at the end of November and while Douglas admitted that his visit had cheered him up, he wrote to Adey "unknown to Bobbie, to beg you to do what you can for me with Oscar" as Adey was due to visit Oscar. By the time this letter reached Adey he had already paid his visit to Reading gaol and the letter distressed him "for I can say so little to comfort you and I would do all I can. .... You must not think that I do not know what Oscar's change towards you must be to you, but Robbie will tell you that from the very first I never believed that it was more than a passing delirium of gaol moral fever".

Ross left Douglas in January 1896; Ross had grown (only for a week) a beard, something only Adey and Charles Ricketts among Wilde's inner circle had ever done with success. Adey had apparently grown his as soon as he was able and kept it, as far as we know, all his life.

Sybil Queensberry continued to use Adey as an intermediary, sending music books and a pair of shoes via him to her son, although Adey's next visit seems to have been delayed until June 1896. He does not appear to have returned, despite promising to do so, by the time Douglas sent an exasperated letter in late September which begins:

> My dear More, I know quite well that you are not a traitor to my interests, and have never had such a thought about you. At the same time I think that you as well as most other of Oscar's and my friends in London have quite forgotten all the old traditions and conditions of my friendship with Oscar, and you are all very different from yourselves and more like the rest of the world, and (if I may say so without offence) more English than you used to be.

Douglas had presumably thought of Adey, with his knowledge of languages and experience of travel, as cosmopolitan in his outlook. He asked Adey to intercede on his behalf with the Leversons who he had heard had "abused" him, and ended with "love to Bobbie". Still worrying about the Leversons at the end of October, Douglas promised Adey "a copy of my poems as soon as I get them". When he did get them he gave Adey one of the twenty copies "sur hollande" inscribed on the recto of the English half-title page (the poems were printed in English and French) "More Adey from his friend the Author. November 1896. Alfred Douglas P.T.O. Naples X" and on the recto of the French half-title page "To More from Bosie, November 1896".[18] The book had already made its way into a collector's library and from there to the sale-room by 1921. Douglas had also given Adey an inscribed copy of his first, anonymous, book *The City of the Soul*.

Adey visited Wilde in July; Wilde had petitioned the Home Secretary for this meeting, saying that

> Mr More Adey is anxious to see him on behalf of Mrs Oscar Wilde with reference to coming to some agreement with regard to the guardianship, education, and future of their children, and also with regard to financial arrangements connected with their marriage settlements

The Home Office allowed this to be a private meeting.

When Adey wrote to Wilde in September he began with news of Ross and Miss Schuster before turning to what must have been business agreed in July. There is a suggestion that he had not fully understood Wilde's wishes:

> Acting on advice I have just written to the Home Secretary, undertaking, if you are released before May, to accompany you abroad at once, and promising that you will remain there until after the end of May. I hope I did right.

He told Wilde that he had written to Constance but that Wilde should seek permission to write to her himself. There followed a strange sentence which betrayed both insecurity and, perhaps, foreboding about Wilde's reactions to what Ross and Adey were planning on his behalf:

> If you should hear of anything that I have done on your behalf without your knowledge of which you do not approve, I trust you will repudiate it in as strong terms as you please.

While Adey said that he had written to the Home Secretary, his letter was never posted as he received at about the same time a letter from the Home Office saying that there were no grounds for an early release.

Sidney Hargrove, Constance's family solicitor, had originally proposed that what remained of the Wildes' property following the Tite Street sale should be secured for the benefit of Cyril and Vyvyan. His proposal assumed the Wildes would divorce, but Constance's refusal led Hargrove to devise another plan which would have annulled the bankruptcy.

Hargrove's plan would have meant that Blacker and Clifton, as trustees of the marriage settlement, would have withdrawn their claim, reducing creditors' claims to an amount which Ross and Adey believed they would be able to raise from friends and sympathisers.

Unfortunately, the only one among Wilde's close advisers who should have known better – Arthur Clifton – now interfered. Wilde had said to Adey, "I hope Arthur will come and bring me good news of you and Robbie" and, as co-trustee, Clifton had been allowed an interview with Wilde at the beginning of October 1896; as he subsequently told Blacker:

> As to business matters, he did not express any very decided opinion but thought he ought to be left something out of the settlement if possible, and I told him what I thought would be a good plan – namely that he should retain about a third of his life interest: and I told him I would do my best to see that that was arranged.
>
> As I told you Mrs Wilde, whom I saw immediately after, quite agreed so there ought to be little difficulty.[19]

Clifton's woeful ignorance of relevant law is shown in his throw-away remark about the life interest. For Wilde to retain such an interest was contrary to the law and, as Robert Maguire says:

> The ill-conceived idea, which apparently originated with Clifton in the impromptu manner suggested by his letter, was eventually, under the equally uncomprehending advocacy of More Adey, to poison relations between Oscar and Constance Wilde, with fatal results for the reconciliation both ardently desired.[20]

Blacker had taken Clifton's word for the ease with which his suggestion could be implemented and Hargrove, clearly irritated by their intervention, came up with yet another proposal. Under this, Constance would pay the official receiver £50 for a one third interest in the marriage settlement; she would then be free to settle this on her husband.

With the Home Secretary's refusal to commute his sentence Wilde was more depressed than at any time since entering prison, and in entirely the wrong frame of mind to have to deal with the ill-informed but well-intentioned efforts of his friends. It may not be possible to construct a coherent picture of the discussions and correspondence because letters are missing and conversations were not recorded; much of it seems in any case to have led to misunderstandings. Clifton wrote to Adey at the end of November for news because he was feeling "out in the cold", but as he had already complained that entertaining friends had prevented him from working on the draft petition Adey had sent him, he was clearly being of little help.

Sidney Hargrove, even more frustrated than he had been at Clifton's intervention, wrote to Wilde in mid-December and Wilde immediately wrote to Adey reporting Hargrove's letter and – for the last time during this particular saga – putting his faith in Adey:

> I feel that I had better trust myself entirely to your judgment, and I am now of opinion that your course was a wise one.

Adey's "course" had been for Wilde's friends to offer the Receiver £50 for Wilde's interest in the marriage settlement. Hargrove's letter had told Wilde that unless that offer was withdrawn, Constance's offer for that interest would be withdrawn. Constance was more ill than Wilde or his friends knew and was concerned, probably correctly given his financial history, that Wilde would not act responsibly towards Cyril and Vyvyan in the event of her death. Wilde thought:

> my wife's proposal that in case of my surviving her I was to have £150 a year was, I think, a cruel and heartless one, and as

inconsiderate of the children's interest as of my existence.

The dealings over the marriage settlement were to be one source of Wilde's anger with Adey and Ross; the other was to be the amount of money available to Wilde on his release, about which he had unrealistic expectations, fed by Adey's vagueness about the true state of his finances.

> If my wife leaves me absolutely without a penny I can only trust that for a year at any rate I will be looked after.

Wilde must have felt that Adey and Ross were perhaps not following his wishes as closely as he would have liked for, when he wrote to Messrs Stoker and Hansell on the last day of 1896, appointing them as his solicitors, he could not have been clearer:

> I believe I am correct in stating that the general outlines of the matter at issue have been communicated, by or through Mr More Adey, to you, but I am anxious, for your guidance and satisfaction, as well as for my own, that my own wishes and views should be clearly conveyed to you under my own hand.

He continued in this letter to argue over financial matters and towards the end gave a further hint of exasperation with Adey

> Would you kindly ask Mr More Adey to use all his efforts to see me here *himself*. I have much to talk to him about. Also tell him that I *quite* understand that the books were a present from my friend Mr Humphreys the publisher.

The fact of Wilde conveying these thoughts through a third party could be because his freedom to send letters was limited, but he got his way when Adey visited on 28 January.

On that visit Adey had clearly interceded on Douglas's behalf but Douglas was not fulsome in his thanks:

> Thanks for your letter. I am obliged to you for what you have done, but you must forgive me if I cannot get myself into the state of extravagant gratitude which you seem rather to think is due to you for doing what I cannot but think was simply what was to be expected of you. If, after eighteen months, you have ventured to remonstrate mildly with Oscar about his cruel and insulting unkindness to me and the misery he has made me suffer for no cause whatever, I don't think it is more than I have a right to expect from anyone who is my friend, and I do not think you need to distress yourself about having made this concession to what you call your own 'better judgment', but which I prefer to think of as other people's worse judgment.

After blaming Ross and Adey's behaviour on "the baleful influence of the Catholic Church" and "Popish weakness coupled with social cowardice", Douglas closed with:

> Forgive what seems harsh and disagreeable in this letter. My nerves are much unstrung by this incident, and you know I am truly fond of you, dear More, and appreciate your kindness, though your ways are not my ways and I can't see with your eyes.

Four weeks after the January visit Adey was back at Reading, accompanied by Ross and Ernest Leverson. This time Wilde had been promised a private room and he looked forward to the meeting in a letter to Adey:

> We shall then surely be able to discuss all business matters. Business with you, seriousness with Ernest, nonsense with Robbie.

What happened in the meeting is not known, but only a week later Wilde wrote to Adey to say:

> My business is I know unpleasant, but then it was not for pleasure that you took its burden on you. .... Your news has distressed me a good deal.

This letter is long and rancorous, and is particularly hard on the Queensberry family's refusal to meet the Marquess's claim on Wilde, thus avoiding bankruptcy. Although he signs himself "Your affectionate friend", Wilde admits, "I fear you see traces of bitterness in my business letters. Yes, that is so. It is very terrible."

On 1 April Wilde wrote to Ross giving instructions for the treatment of the letter to Douglas now known as *De Profundis*. He had intended to send Ross the manuscript at the same time but the prison authorities would not allow it to leave the prison until Wilde's release. The letter to Ross underlines the relationship between Ross and Adey:

> As soon as you, and of course More Adey whom I always include with you, have read it, I want you to have it carefully copied for me.

It also appears to recognise that the relationship between Adey and Douglas is different to that between Ross and Douglas because although Wilde makes Ross responsible for having the manuscript typed and copied, once verified, "the original should be dispatched to A.D. by More".

The remainder of this letter directed blame at Ross ("I have got to blame you, and I am far too fond of you to blame you to anyone else") and, to a lesser extent, Adey for underestimating Hargrove and failing to ensure that there was no "discord being made between myself and my wife on such a subject as money". As money had been the chief, and for most of the time only bone of contention this seems unfair but the accusation was focused on Ross and Adey's decision to bid against Constance for the life interest. This was ill-judged but had been fuelled by Wilde's stated desire to receive more than had been offered by Constance and her advisers.

The letter ends with an extraordinary and lengthy section on Wilde's fur coat in which he expresses his anger at his brother Willie and Willie's wife Lily. Lily had corresponded with Adey during the period of Wilde's imprisonment and he had probably interceded with Wilde on her behalf when she was very short of money. Wilde had given her £50 from the money Ernest Leverson was holding for him and clearly felt that she showed insufficient gratitude. The relationship between the brothers was non-existent by this time but Lily had visited Wilde in Wandsworth and was throughout much more sympathetic towards him than was her husband. She and Adey seem to have got on well and she told him her side of the fur coat story. Wilde believed he had given the coat and other clothes to Willie for safe keeping; Lily was certain that he had told them to do what they liked with everything except his shirts, which Lily carefully preserved when Willie sold everything else.[21] There is a certain irony here; after Willie's death, Lily married Alexander Teixeira de Mattos who wrote in a letter to a friend in 1917, "I have ordered eight new coloured shirts, bringing the total up to 23. Then I have about a dozen black-and-white shirts; and only seven dress-shirts, I find. This makes 42 in all. My father's theory was that no gentleman should have fewer than eighty shirts to his name".

Five days later Wilde wrote again to Ross "partly because I have to blame you" and goes over similar ground about the marriage settlement and divorce. Wilde referred Ross to a letter he had written to Adey which was sent the following day.[22]

Wilde's letter to Adey has much that is similar to those to Ross, opening with "I have been thrust into a very false position by my friends, and have to suffer for it. I see nothing now but to submit, and to return beforehand my life-interest as a sort of parting-gift, so as not to leave my exit from the marriage-tie too ignominious and unworthy". Wilde told Ross and Adey to read each other's letters and consider "the position into which I have been led". Divorce seemed the only course, but it would mean breaking "entirely every link with my children".

The remainder of this letter reinforced Adey's position as the chief go-between with the Queensberry family and with the Leversons. Wilde's mood towards Douglas remained as it had been in *De Profundis*, and Adey was tasked with giving the other Queensberry family members the "facts" and getting Percy to provide the money he had promised. Ernest Leverson was the subject of an attack over his handling of the £1000 entrusted to him by Wilde, who had clearly been brooding on what his financial position would be on his release. The attack was unjust and Leverson answered the charges in full the following month. Among Adey's papers in the Clark are notes on Leverson's accounting which must have come from discussions following Wilde's letter.

Adey's relationship with Ernest Leverson may have been business-like and tested by Wilde's fears about Leverson's actions, but his relationship with Ada was very friendly. At the beginning of Wilde's problems she addressed him as dear Mr Adey, but was already on "Bobbie" terms with Ross. But before long she was sending Adey her parodies from *Punch* and sympathising when Adey had been shaken by an "accident in a cab". She seemed often to have the company of Ross, Turner ("with a friend") and Adey at her home. By July 1896 she went so far as to sign herself "Sphinx" and added "We thought your French friend charming & he dined with us at the "Lyric", he is most sympathetic". There is no clue as to who this might be. Adding to Adey's constant stream of illnesses and accidents at the beginning of 1896 he – in Ada's words – "compromised yourself with a chair".

In letters to his solicitors later in April Wilde accepted Constance's terms and began planning what he would do following his release. Careless of what solicitors might charge, Wilde gave Hansell a number of instructions to convey to Adey including acquiring a *Murray's Guide* for the area around Finisterre. Suddenly aware of costs, at the end of the letter Wilde suggests Hansell should send the letter to Adey (who would return it), thus saving copying!

Whether Hansell did as requested is not clear, but on 1 May Wilde wrote to Adey to complain that he did not know whether his letters were reaching Hansell or, if they were, whether they were acted upon.

Adey and Ross were about to visit Wilde and Charles Ricketts was to accompany them. Wilde had acceded to Ricketts' request for a visit but now regretted it as he wanted to "talk of other matters than books". He asked Adey to write out his business affairs because

> I read better than I listen, and your handwriting is hieratic in its clearness and style.

Others may have thought Adey vague, but on paper he could express himself well, even if he was given to verbosity.

It is in this letter that Wilde said

> I do not know whether Wotton-under-Edge is the name of a town or of your mother's place, so I send this to Hornton Street to be forwarded

This is the best indication we have that local folklore about Wilde visiting Adey in Gloucestershire is wishful thinking.

A week later Wilde wrote again with very detailed requests for clothes and toiletries for his release, all to be purchased from £25 Adela Schuster had provided through Adey.

The meeting with Ross, Adey and Ricketts – "painful and unsatisfactory" according to Wilde – took place the following week. The circle of friends around Wilde in the early nineties is often thought of as homogenous, but when Ricketts met Ross and Adey at Reading station prior to the visit he remembered

> Our manner at this meeting was constrained, we were almost strangers and our behaviour resembled that of men about to attend a funeral, Ross even developing a touch of hysteria on reaching the Prison gate.

In fact he had "known Ross only by name" until he came to tell Ricketts that the visit to Wilde had been arranged. We can be confident that he did not know Adey at all. Ross and Adey saw Wilde first and when Ricketts was allowed in to the interview room

> There was constraint upon the faces of my fellow-visitors. Later I was to learn that Wilde had been difficult, arrogant and unreasonable, impatient with all arrangements, and utterly rebellious to all proposals for his immediate future, though long since discussed and agreed upon. Of this nothing was visible, his cordial greeting and enquiries might have been spoken in Bond Street, in a new frock coat with a large button hole, not here and in the drab garment with the black arrows of a prison uniform.[23]

Two or three days after the visit, Ricketts wrote to Adey after talking to Frank Harris about Wilde's money troubles:

> I have seen my lawyers in the matter of raising a small sum & I think I can promise £100 in the space of two or three weeks. This

> I think you can safely reckon on though the date is somewhat uncertain since mortgaging has to be gone into & this I do not understand. ... Of course, I don't want Oscar to know anything about this matter of mine. It would be very unwise.[24]

Ross knew how poor Ricketts and his partner Shannon were and ensured that, after Wilde's death his estate repaid the money.

The "painful and unsatisfactory" meeting was followed by equally painful letters from Wilde. In the letters to Ross and Adey all Wilde's confusion and anger about their management of his affairs was laid out. He was much harder on Adey in the letter to Ross than he was to Adey directly. While he castigated Adey, he continued to ask him to undertake tasks for him and his description of Adey shows exactly why people were attracted to him as a friend:

> My dear More, the time is come when you should recognise one thing: that is that in all business matters even of the simplest kind your judgment is utterly incompetent, your opinion either foolish or perverted, and your capacity to understand the most ordinary circumstances of actual life absolutely nil. You are a man of singular culture: of grave and castigated taste in style: you can discern the intellectual architecture of work that seems to others flamboyant or fantastic by an immediate sympathy of recognition: to discern the classical element in contemporary work is your function, one that you should more fully recognise than you do. You have not in literature ever tried to do yourself justice. In your nature you are most sympathetic. You would love to help others. You are patient to excess. Your forbearance is beautiful. But you have not enough common sense to manage the affairs of a tom-tit in a hedge. Robbie is better as a guide, for if he is quite irrational he has the advantage of being always illogical, so he occasionally comes to a right conclusion. But you not merely are equally irrational, but are absolutely logical: you start always from the wrong premises, and arrive logically at the wrong conclusion.

To Ross, Wilde said:

> You and my other friends have so little imagination, so little sympathy, so little power of appreciating what was beautiful, noble, lovely, and of good report that you can think of nothing better – you, More Adey and, I am told, your brother Aleck – than to rush in between us with an entirely ignorant solicitor and part us first and then make mischief between us.

Of the use of Wilde's money, "I, and not More Adey, am the proper judge of what is for my use", and the advice given to him by Adey "not to surrender your legal rights over your wife and your children" Wilde dismisses as "absurd nonsense". Everything Adey and "my friends" have done Wilde considers a betrayal of his wishes and, speaking of Douglas, he says (with an odd echo of Jack in *The Importance of Being Earnest*)

> now that I reflect on your conduct and More Adey's to me in this matter I feel I have been unjust to that unfortunate young man.

In much the same way as in his letter to Adey quoted above, Wilde recited to Ross Adey's qualities:

> He is cultivated. He is sympathetic. He is kind. He is patient. He is gentle. He is affectionate. He is full of charming emotional qualities.

Knowing that Ross would share the letter with Adey he went on to say some enormously hurtful things:

> in matters of business he is the most solemn donkey that ever stepped. He has neither memory, nor understanding, nor capacity to realise a situation, or appreciate a point. His gravity of manner makes his entire folly mask as wisdom. Every one is taken in. He is so serious in manner that one believes he can form an intellectual opinion. He can't. He is *extremely dense* in all matters requiring lucidity or imagination or instinct. In business matters he is *stupid*. The harm he has done me is irreparable, and he is as pleased as possible with himself. Now I have realised this, I feel it right, Robbie, that you should know it. If you have ever thought him sensible, give up the idea. He is incapable, as I have written to him, of managing the domestic affairs of a tom-tit in a hedge for a single afternoon. He is a *stupid man*, in practical concerns.

It was probably at about this time that Adey, looking for other ways of securing funds for Wilde after his release, approached Frank Harris, who recalled:

> He promised to send me the book "De Profundis" as soon as it was finished. Just before his release his friend, Mr. More Adey, called upon me and wanted to know whether I would publish Oscar's work. I said I would. He then asked me what I would give for it. I told him I didn't want to make anything out of Oscar and would give him as much as I could, rehearsing the proposal I had made to Oscar. Thereupon he told me Oscar would prefer a fixed price. I thought the answer extraordinary and the gentle, urbane manner of Mr. More Adey, whom I hardly knew at that time and misunderstood, got on my nerves. I replied curtly that

before I could state a price, I'd have to see the work, adding at the same time that I had wished to do Oscar a good turn, but, if he could find another publisher, I'd be delighted. Mr. More Adey assured me that there was nothing in the book to which any prude even could object, no *arrière pensée* of any kind, and so forth and so on. I answered with a jest, a wretched play on his French phrase.

Here is more evidence that Adey had previously kept apart from many in Wilde's circle. Getting on Frank Harris's nerves was not difficult, but Adey's clear lack of understanding of business supports Wilde's view of him.

Although it had been planned for some time that Adey would meet Wilde from prison – he had been hoping to be released from Reading rather than having to return to Pentonville where he began his sentence – Wilde now asked Reggie Turner to meet him and told Adey that in the light of Ross and Adey's behaviour he could not face them.

> If after a week you care to come to Havre and give me some explanation, I shall be delighted to see you. I hope Robbie will come with you.

Later in the day, and in the same letter he said

> Of course I really will be glad to see you in the morning of my release, and I know you have taken a great deal of trouble about it. So come either to the prison with Reggie or to his rooms if that is more convenient. But we must not talk about business.

The duality of his feelings for Adey resurfaced here; after telling him that he "would find little pleasure in my society. I feel so bitterly about so many things" he recognised

> Your intentions were always good and kind: your heart was always ready to vibrate in true sympathy: but your judgment was wrong: and the worse the results the worse your advice got. It was a miracle I escaped the divorce, the exile, the entire abandonment.
>
> However, for your real heart-actions, your unwearying good nature, and desire to help me, I thank you very deeply. In a week I hope to be in a sweeter mood and to have lost some of my present bitterness. Then let us meet and talk about literature, in which your instinct is always right, your judgment castigated and serene, your sympathies intellectual.

Although Wilde had wanted Turner to meet him, it was in the end Headlam and Adey who had the carriage waiting outside Pentonville prison. Turner wrote to say that Wilde would be in good hands and, in what must have been another blow to Wilde, that Turner's allowance would have been stopped had his "people" heard he was meeting Wilde. He then mounted a passionate defence of Ross and Adey, admitting that mistakes had been made but that neither Ross nor Adey was responsible for them and that they had done "great things" for Wilde "for so long and so unostentatiously".

The carriage arrived at Headlam's house in Upper Bedford Place before 6am and there were discussions about what was to happen next, followed by what must have been an uncomfortable meeting with the Leversons, given that Wilde was still not convinced that Leverson had acted properly in respect of Wilde's money. Finally, it was Adey who accompanied Wilde on the train to Newhaven and on the ferry *La Tamise* overnight to Dieppe.

Having arrived in Dieppe, Wilde asked Adey to write to Major Nelson, the governor at Reading gaol to let him know of Wilde's safe arrival in France. Wilde would later write himself at some length.

Once Wilde had been released from prison and it was clear to Douglas that it was thought that any meeting between him and Wilde would have disastrous consequences for Wilde, the letters to Adey and Ross took on a different tone. He blamed Adey "for the agreement under which Oscar has been placed in the ridiculous and ignominious position" and sought an explanation as to Adey's views and the "steps you propose to take to free Oscar (and myself) from the ridiculously transparent Jewish trap which has been laid for him by the admirable George Lewis, and into which you have guided him". In response to a "rather absurd" letter from Ross, which presumably gave news of another of Adey's illnesses, Douglas said:

> Nothing short of a very serious operation can atone for More's part in the sale of Oscar's freedom to the Jews. A mere feverish cold is no good at all. But operations cover a multitude of sins as you know, or ought to.

Ross replied that he (Ross) must have lost his sense of humour "or has Count Mather's green electricity deprived you of all sense of decency?". Douglas told Adey he could receive no more letters from Ross and could not remain friends with him. At the same time he expressed surprise that Ross should have thought his previous letters carried any insult towards Adey: "Nothing could be further from my wish". His next letter to Adey suggests that Adey had distanced himself from Ross's criticisms of Douglas. Without Adey's side of the correspondence it is impossible to know how much of what Douglas says is his (mis)interpretation of Adey's position. In all this correspondence there appears to be considerable misunderstanding on all sides but there also seems to have been little co-ordination between Ross and Adey in their dealings with Douglas. The correspondence is untraceable from the middle of July until October when Douglas pleaded with Adey for news. He wrote at considerable length about his reasons for being "obliged to quarrel with and break definitely with Bobbie" but he hopes that "anyhow you and I may remain friends".

Like everything else about Adey, Bosie's letters raise more questions than they answer. In 1897 Bosie took Adey to task for apparently publishing some animal poems which too closely resembled Bosie's own efforts. These animal poems have not surfaced, and they sound unlikely in the light of Adey's usual output, but Adey's side of the correspondence is also absent.

Notes

1 This chapter quotes extensively from Wilde's letters from prison contained in *The Complete Letters of Oscar Wilde*, edited by Merlin Holland and Rupert Hart-Davis, Fourth Estate 2000

2 *On Moral Courage*, Compton Mackenzie, Collins 1962, p. 67

3 *Oscar Wilde*, Richard Ellmann, Hamish Hamilton 1987, p. 438

4 *Stewart Headlam: A Biography*, F G Bettany, John Murray 1926 p. 130

5 *Memories of a Misspent Youth 1872-1896*, Grant Richards, Heinemann 1932. p. 339. Richards's says of the Crown, "The occasional frequenters one could number by the score. Hubert Crackanthorpe, Rothenstein, Beardsley, Oscar – but not very often – Robert Ross, Percy Addleshaw, Lionel Johnson, John Lane (observant and not at all in his element), John Gray, Conder, Stewart Headlam, Victor Plarr, Max Beerbohm, Kains Jackson, Theodore Wratislaw."

6 *Letters to the Sphinx from Oscar Wilde*, Ada Leverson, Duckworth 1930, p. 45

7 *Stewart Headlam's Radical Anglicanism*, John Richard Orens, University of Illinois Press 2003, p. 37

8 *Stenbock, Yeats and the Nineties*, John Adlard, Cecil & Amelia Woolf 1969, p. 82

9 *Wales England Wed*, Ernest Rhys, Dent 1940, p. 162

10 *Morning Post* 13 August 1895

11 *Constance: The Tragic and Scandalous Life of Mrs Oscar Wilde*, Franny Moyle, John Murray 2011, p. 259

12 Constance Wilde to Adey, 3 August 1896, William Andrews Clark Library

13 William Wilde to Adey, 9 February 1896, William Andrews Clark Library

14 The story of Wilson and his pamphlet is told in 'Some Gentle Criticisms of British Justice' in *Oscar Wilde: Myths, Miracles and Imitations*, John Stokes, Cambridge University Press 1996

15 *Ceremonies of Bravery*, J Robert Maguire, Oxford University Press 2013

16 Fr Sebastien Bowden to Adey, 9 June 1895, Magdalen College

17 Johnson to Adey, 13 July 1895. Quoted in *Some Letters of Lionel Johnson*, Raymond Roseliep. Unpublished thesis, Department of English, Notre Dame, Indiana 1953.

18 Item 147A in the catalogue of "The Sporting Library of Mr William Brewster of New York City", The Anderson Galleries, 1921

19 Maguire, p. 59

20 Maguire, p. 60

21 Little attention has been paid to Lily Wilde, but the story of her dealings with Wilde is told in 'Lily Wilde and Oscar's Fur Coat', Kevin O'Brien in *The Journal of the Eighteen Nineties Society*, No. 21, 1994

22 Merlin Holland suggests that the 1 April letter may have been withheld by the prison authorities which is why the 6 April letter appears to cover so much of the same ground.

23 *Oscar Wilde: Recollections*, Jean Paul Raymond and Charles Ricketts, The Nonesuch Press 1932, p. 45-46

24 Quoted in *Charles Ricketts: A Biography*, J G P Delaney, Oxford University Press 1990, p. 110

5. DIEPPE AND AFTER

Adey, Ross and Turner did not stay long with Wilde in France and, once he was alone his thoughts turned once again to Douglas. At the end of May Wilde told Adey that he "could not say to you one hundredth part of the gratitude and affection I feel for you". Adey sent books over the summer but was, as always, not well. Wilde wanted Ross and Adey to visit in July but wondered if Adey would be well enough. By October, when Wilde was with Douglas in Naples it "is ages since I heard from you, and Robbie's statement that you had become a country gentleman was bewildering". Adey had presumably retreated to Wotton under Edge to recuperate from the excitement of the prison years and the trip to France. Wilde's view of Adey's business acumen had undergone a swift transformation because in the same letter he asks him to "fling yourself at once" into influencing Pinker (the American literary agent) over the "current price of poetry in America". Wilde was trying to get *The Ballad of Reading Gaol* published in America.

Just over a month later the relationship changed once again. Wilde was in Posilippo. Around the 19th of the month he received a letter from Adey which confirmed that Douglas was, for the purposes of Constance's continuing financial support, a "disreputable person". He then wrote to Reggie Turner castigating Ross and Adey who had both "played an incomprehensible part in the affair". At much the same time he wrote letters to Ross and Adey. To Ross he wrote a few paragraphs about the composition of *The Ballad* and then turned to the "disreputable person" situation. He had written to the solicitor Hansell "violently" and of "dear More I have made a holocaust: it had to be. But he will survive any pyre: in the ashes his heart – cor cordium – will be found untouched".[1]

There is a long letter from Adey to Wilde in early January 1898[2] in which he says that "if I had anything to forgive you, I have forgiven it long ago. It is very nice of our common friends to defend me, often, I dare say, when they may really think that I have done or written something foolish, but, though I am grateful to them, I do not believe in the efficacy of vicarious justification". Sometimes Adey's convoluted phrasing makes it only too clear how misunderstandings could arise from his correspondence. This letter ends with an entreaty to "write soon about beautiful plays and poems and nice new friends and your plans".

In February 1898, with everything apparently forgiven and forgotten, Wilde was in Paris and wanted Adey to visit, "but I suppose that is difficult".

That is not explained, nor is the odd coda to the letter which reads:

> Are you writing?
>
> Are you in love?
>
> Are you happy? Ever yours

There is then a gap of more than a year before the next extant letter from Wilde to Adey, who had clearly just received a presentation copy of *The Importance of Being Earnest*. Wilde was staying in Gland, Switzerland and the letter is much more positive than previous ones to Adey, finishing with a touching paragraph:

> I often think of your wonderful visits to me when I was in pain, and of your tenderness, and kindness to me. I fear that, in consequence, your stay in the Purgatorio – where the poets are – will be too brief.

Before leaving Switzerland for Italy in April, Wilde invited Ross to visit him in Genoa bemoaning the fact that he never sees him, "And there is More, who is apparently sentenced to life-long imprisonment in Great Britain: cannot he get away? I should love to have you both near at hand for a little. It would be delightful." This is followed by the slightly barbed thought that at Easter "one is supposed to forgive all one's friends".

Only one more letter from Wilde to Adey survives, written from Rome in April 1900. Ross had told Wilde of the death of Adey's mother and Wilde expressed his "great regret":

> You were so kind to *my* mother, so sympathetic and gentle in your delicate attention to her up to the last, that I know you will let me express my sorrow at the death of *your* mother: it seems to me that I have almost a right to do so: for friends have all things in common.

At about the same time he wrote to Ross thanking him for letting him know about Adey's loss and expressing the hope he will see Adey in the Vatican dressed in Spanish Renaissance fashion – "All the people at the Vatican try to look like More: that they succeed is their fault rather than his". That he was already known for a dark and sombre style of dress makes later attempts to link his style with his mental condition even less credible.

There is no sign of Adey between then and Wilde's death at the end of November. As he did not attend the funeral it is reasonable to suppose that he was once again in poor health. Adey sent a wreath and among his papers in the Clark is a very detailed list in his hand (and in French) of the expenses of the funeral, although there is no indication that Adey contributed to the costs.

One explanation for Adey's invisibility around this time is the death of his mother in April 1900. He was very close to his mother and the combination of her death and his inheritance of a considerable property would have kept him in Wotton under Edge. It appears that Clifton may have been acting as Adey's solicitor in respect of his mother's estate; this is odd given the family's close connection with Jotcham's, the solicitors in Wotton under Edge. Jotcham's acted on Adey's behalf when he was committed in 1925. As shown in the following chapter, there were also developments around the Carfax Gallery which would have involved Adey. But there is no correspondence or other papers to demonstrate what he was doing.

In April 1902 Douglas wrote from Shaftesbury:

> My dear More
>
> Just a line to say I am here in case you have any news. However unless it is really necessary that I should know I would rather hear nothing more at all, as it is so agitating & I am overwhelmed with other worries. Please let me know what I owe you for Frank. I am really ashamed to have given you so much trouble.[3]

Frank here appears to be a young man for whom Douglas had asked Adey to find employment, but Douglas had been using him as a valet during a stay in Scotland and seemed to think he needed no other job. What the other news was for which Douglas was waiting is not known.

In the same week Douglas wrote:

> My dear More
>
> I enclose a cheque for £12. No news of interest. I shall be up in London before long. Tell Bobbie we are sorry we missed seeing him. Yours ever Bosie

If £12 was payment "for Frank", Adey must have gone to considerable trouble!

"We" here refers to Douglas and his new wife, the poet Olive Custance; they had married a month earlier. It is not clear whether Adey knew Olive before this but they were certainly good friends after the marriage, with Olive sending him poems and photographs from abroad. The friendship remained strong and in 1910 Adey rushed to a nursing home when he heard that Olive had gone in for an operation and reported to Douglas how pleased he was that she was recovering well.

One event in 1905 involving Adey and Douglas has been recorded, and has a clear bearing on Douglas's behaviour in the years following. Compton Mackenzie, then a young novelist recorded it in his diary and then felt the occasion important enough to repeat in two of his books[4]

> In the spring of 1905 I was at Ross's house in Hornton Street, Kensington, on the evening of the day that the first edition of *De Profundis* was published. There were present also Lord Alfred Douglas, Reginald Turner and More Adey. ... Ross was reading some of the letters he had been receiving about the book. I recall only two of these. There was one from Bernard Shaw commenting on the ability of Wilde to pose even in prison and there was another from George Alexander in which he said that the book had made him shed tears. ... While Ross was reading the letters that evening Alfred Douglas was fidgeting and scratching himself with his back to the fire, standing on the fender from time to time and sliding off it with an irritating clang. Reginald Turner and More Adey probably already knew that Ross had not published the part of *De Profundis* which blamed Alfred Douglas for so much of what had happened, but of course I was unaware of this at the time and when Douglas began to criticise Wilde's manner of life in Paris after he was released from prison I remember feeling embarrassed by the sudden change in the atmosphere of that room in Hornton Street. Then Ross said something which particularly annoyed Douglas who slid off the fender, kicked it with a crash, and strode out of the room. Presently he came back in his astrakhan-collared great-coat and standing in the doorway said, "You don't know what you're talking about, Robbie." With this he slammed the door behind him and left the house.

Adey, and perhaps Turner, would at this time have been living in the same house as Ross and it is therefore unlikely that they would not have known the story of the *De Profundis* manuscript.

For the time being Adey continued to be friends with Douglas and his wife, and contributed to *The Academy* while Douglas was editor. It can only have been that it was edited by his old friend that Adey associated himself with *The Academy*, although during Douglas's editorship it managed to acquire a distinguished list of contributors. But in those years between 1907 and 1910 progress was not smooth. W Sorley Brown, in his biography of Douglas's associate, T W H Crosland says of the magazine that it

> purported to be "an independent, uncommercial journal conducted in the interest of literature and for the maintenance

> of a high standard of fearless and independent criticism." And there can be no question that The Academy was so conducted, and that the standard of fearless and independent criticism was maintained in a manner which had not been surpassed, if equalled, in the history of English literary papers. Douglas and Crosland between them succeeded in making The Academy the most candid, most readable, and most admirable literary paper in the United Kingdom.

This candour "gained them some loyal admirers and many enemies".[5]

One of those enemies was Robert Ross, who had been a frequent contributor under the editorship of Douglas's predecessor. Following interference by Crosland with a review Ross had written, Douglas and Ross fell out and Ross contributed no more. It was only after this that Adey began contributing, showing once again the conflicted nature of Adey's friendships.

On 8 June 1907 Adey contributed two translations of poems, "Imitation from 'A morte de Don Joao'" from the Portuguese of Guerra Junqueiro, and "Le Ciel est Par-dessus le Toit" from the French of Paul Verlaine and a drama review "Maitre des Illusions de la Vie". A further poetic translation "Imitation from Maurice Maeterlinck" appeared on 25 January 1908 and the following month a drama review of "'The Sicilian Players". "Maitre des Illusions de la Vie" was a review of J E Vedrenne and Granville Barker's staging of the "Don Juan in Hell" scene from Shaw's *Man and Superman* at the Court Theatre, where, four years later, Adey's translation of Ibsen's *Brand* was to have its first performance. Adey knew how to flatter an audience:

> The whole play at one sitting would tax too much even the audience of the Court Theatre. Without claiming for this audience greater intelligence than that of other theatres, it is at least especially interested in the newer and untried developments of the stage, and especially *amateur*, of the Intellectual Drama.

And he knew how to flatter his friends:

> Mr Shaw is self-sufficient; he is driven to co-operation only by his medium of expression. He has found the only artist capable of interpreting him in the *mise en scène*, an artist in the plastic modes of Art as encyclopædic as himself, and in a sense as protæan. There is scarcely a genus of Art in which this artist's immense ability has not already proved itself formative. No name is printed on the programmes, but the *aside* has passed out of date, and it is impossible to conceal his identity. ..... write

> Mr Charles Ricketts's name as large upon the piece as that of the author himself. Here is another addition to the attractions of the Court on which to congratulate Messrs Vedrenne and Barker.

Charles Ricketts was a Carfax artist, having exhibited bronzes there in 1906 and drawings in 1907. His partner Charles Shannon also exhibited there.

The review of the Sicilian Players – a troupe from Sicily performing at the Shaftesbury Theatre – was a meditation on the importance of Realism "in the intellectual consideration of the drama".

> My object is, to urge those who have been deterred from seeing the Sicilians by their reputation for Realism, to take their courage in their hands and go at once, while Signora Mimi Aguglia is here to interpret it.

Several hundred words later, Adey ended an extremely positive review with a very unprofessional apology:

> These remarks are obviously not those of a professed Dramatic Critic. They are founded on the plays that I have seen. I have not seen Juan Jose, Russida, La Lupa, nor, of course, Feudalismo, which is produced on Friday the 28th. A study of these might modify my opinions.

In the next issue of *The Academy*, a letter to the editor from Robb Lawson[6] began:

> Sir – I was glad to read the appreciation of the Sicilian Players which appeared in your last issue. It is so far removed from the cock-sure methods of the ordinary professional critic as to be a really scientific document. There are so many of these gentlemen lying in wait for the opportunity of explaining a new thrill, that it is pleasant to find one who is anxious to temper his judgment by reason....

None of Adey's contributions to *The Academy* is signed, bearing only the initials M.A.

Not long after these contributions, the relationship between Adey and Douglas was to change, beginning with a letter from Hampstead in May 1910:

> My dear More
>
> I have just ascertained that an almost incredible act of villainy, a mon regard, is about to be or has already been perpetrated by Bobbie Ross. Even against the evidence of my own senses

I would never believe that you could be concerned in such a business nor do I yet altogether believe that R.R. is capable of having done what I am informed he has done. Nevertheless the matter must be cleared up & I beg that you will make an appointment to see me as soon as you conveniently can. If you will come & see me here I can put you up for a night or two, or I will if necessary come to see you at Wooton. Olive is at present in a nursing home, 29 St Georges Road SW. She had an operation about ten days ago & is I am thankful to say going on very well. I hope she will be able to come home next Monday, but she will still have to remain in bed for a week or so after her return.[7]

This was the start of the process leading to the Arthur Ransome trial. Douglas had not been consulted about Ransome's book on Wilde, the first book about him written by someone who had not known him. He was horrified to learn that *De Profundis* had been a letter to him and promptly sued author, publisher and distributor. The real case was against Ross, whom Douglas blamed. Things were already going badly in court for Douglas when Adey was called to give evidence relating to the money given by Douglas to Wilde. Adey's papers in the Clark contain several draft versions of the evidence he felt he could give to the court; the most complete reads:

By request of Lord Alfred Douglas and of his mother, the Marchioness of Queensberry, I undertook in November or early December 1897 to transmit the sum of £200 to Mr Oscar Wilde. I received the said sum of £200 in two instalments, by cheques signed by Lady Queensberry, each for £100 on or about 9 and 18 December 1897, on both of which dates I transmitted £100 to Mr Wilde. One of these sums miscarried and consequently a fresh transmission of £100 was effected by me on 22 January 1898. The whole sum effectively transmitted by me to Mr Wilde on behalf of Lady Q & Lord A.D. was £200.

Lady Queensbury [sic] made the payment of the £200 conditional on Lord Alfred Douglas separating from Mr Wilde.

I cannot deny that as the depository of a fund contributed by admirers of Mr Wilde for his benefit, I indirectly consented during the month of May 1897, under instructions from Mr Wilde, that his residence at any time with Lord Alfred Douglas should constitute a breach of the conditions on which Mrs

Wilde undertook to settle on Mr Wilde an annual allowance of £150.

On Lord Alfred Douglas and Mr Wilde taking up residence together during the latter half of 1897, I represented to both that such residence was contrary to the interests of both.

It was this evidence that led to a severing of relations which Douglas instituted in a typically dramatic letter in April 1913:

Dear More

I see that yesterday when you were recalled by the judge to give evidence you too played the Judas Iscariot to me yr old friend. You deliberately misled the jury. You know perfectly well, for I have discussed the matter with you a dozen times, & you discussed it with my solicitor that the £200 was sent to Wilde in November 1897 within a week of my leaving him at Naples. You also know perfectly well that this £200 formed no part of any "debt of honour". I wish you joy of what you have done knowing as you do that I have for years led a clean straight life & that I have been struggling hard to be a good Christian & a good Catholic & knowing as you also do that Ross, who put up Ransome to write the book, is a filthy beast to this very day an habitual sodomite & corrupter of young boys.

Our friendship is at an end. I shall never speak to you again. It is no business of mine to seek revenge on you or on Ross. But the reckoning will surely come sooner or later.[8]

For the first time in their relationship this letter was signed "Alfred Douglas" rather than Bosie; Douglas sent a copy to the trial judge, Mr Justice Darling at the close of the trial in April. Two months later T W H Crosland was indicted on fourteen counts, the principal one being that he conspired with Lord Alfred Douglas "to pervert justice by falsely accusing Mr Robert Baldwin Ross, the literary executor of Oscar Wilde, of a criminal offence". Crosland's biographer says:

.... shortly after the opening of the proceedings Mr Hayes [defence counsel for Crosland] produced a letter which was sent by Lord Alfred Douglas to Mr Justice Darling at the close of the Ransome case in April. That letter, said Mr Hayes, was handed by the Judge to him and to Mr F E Smith, and when they read it it was entrusted by the Judge to Mr Smith with the suggestion that proceedings for libel should be taken if the party thought it desirable. The letter bore reference to the untrue statement of Ransome in his "Critical Study" of Wilde that Douglas "as soon as there was no money" left Wilde stranded in Naples,

> whereas the established and unassailable truth is that when Douglas left Wilde at his (Douglas's) villa at Naples he gave him £200, which was paid to him through Mr More Adey and Lord Alfred's mother.

Sorley Brown then reprints the letter, omitting the words from "beast" to the end of the first paragraph.[9] At least one newspaper reprinted the letter.

Douglas's various volumes of autobiography make almost no mention of Adey, except where drawing attention to the disputed £200, and making a list of the people who signed the testimonial to Ross in 1908. His feelings about Ross are consistently made clear, but Adey escapes criticism. The only substantive reference is in a piece about Ross in *The Autobiography of Lord Alfred Douglas*, published in 1929:

> His great friend, when I knew him, was Mr More Adey, also at one time a great friend of my own, and after Ross left Church Street, Kensington, he and Adey shared rooms for years in Hornton Street, and afterwards again in another house in Church Street.[10]

So, with the exception of the letter quoted above, Adey seems to have escaped the wrath of Douglas and although he was probably implicitly included in the general condemnation of those around Wilde, there is no attempt to link Adey to the sins of which Douglas accused Ross. In 1925 Reggie Turner wrote to Frank Harris, "I think of all his friends Adey was the one whom Bosie really liked best".

Notes

1 A reference to Shelley's funeral pyre and the inscription on his tomb.

2 The letter only exists as a copy in Adey's hand.

3 1 April 1902, William Andrews Clark Library

4 *On Moral Courage*, Compton Mackenzie, Collins 1962, p. 66

5 Robb Lawson would later write a history of the Scottish theatre.

6 *The Life and Genius of T.W.H.Crosland*, by W Sorley Brown, Cecil Palmer 1928 p.215

7 19 May 1910, William Andrews Clark Library

8 23 April 1923, William Andrews Clark Library

9 Sorley Brown, p. 319

10 *The Autobiography of Lord Alfred Douglas*, Lord Alfred Douglas, Martin Secker 1929, p. 72

Plate 1 Under-the-Hill House, Wotton-under-Edge.

Plate 2 Ibsen's *Brand,* translated by More Adey. Published 1891.

Plate 3 The cover, by Aymer Vallance, of More Adey's translation of *Pastor Sang*, 1893.

Plate 4 The area of the cemetery in Wotton-under-Edge containing More Adey's unmarked grave.

6. THE CARFAX GALLERY

The Carfax Gallery had been established in 1898 by John Fothergill, Edward Perry Warren, William Rothenstein and Arthur Clifton. According to Rothenstein it had been Fothergill who had proposed the idea of a gallery "where Conder's, John's, Sickert's, Orpen's, Max Beerbohm's and my work would be constantly shown".[1] Rothenstein was to be responsible for the choice of art and Arthur Clifton for the business side.

Walter Sickert's younger brother Robert was appointed as administrator. Even his brother recognised the folly of this, telling Rothenstein:

> I have always thought your employing Robert proved your unfitness as a manager[2]

As it was probably Clifton who was responsible for the appointment this seems unfair to Rothenstein.

The gallery was established at 17 Carfax Street, St James's, a street which is still home to art galleries, bookshops and the goods entrance to Christies auction house. Coincidentally, the building now occupied by Christies at the rear of number 17 was, in the early years of the twentieth century, a set of "gentlemen's chambers" overseen by Mrs Lucy Nichols, the wife of H S Nichols, Leonard Smithers's sometime partner and publisher in his own right.

Unlike some of the galleries which were congregating along Bond Street, Carfax did not benefit from top-lighting and large rooms, indeed, reviews tended to refer to the gallery as small or quaint. This was rarely a disadvantage, although one reviewer bemoaned the fact that only glimpses of Rodin's work could be seen:

> I say glimpses, because owing to the size of the gallery, it is small studies and statuettes only that can be seen there.[3]

Although there is still an art gallery at 17 Ryder Street, it is not the same building. The block on that corner of Ryder and Bury Streets was rebuilt in 1909 to a design by G Thrale Jell. There is no description of the gallery as it was in Adey's time but descriptions of exhibitions give some hints. *The Survey of London* says of the block before it was demolished:

> Some Georgian shop-fronts broke the monotony of doors and windows, there being a very fine example on the corner of Ryder and Bury Streets, with round-headed windows between Doric pilasters, and a corner entrance between columns. The backs, however, were a picturesque confusion of plaster-faced gables,

> projecting closet wings of brick or weather boarding, and tall irregular chimney-stacks. [4]

The Doric pilasters did not reach as far as number 17. The building was Georgian and originally a residence. From the one picture we have of the block it must be assumed that the entrance to the gallery was from lower ground floor level, the only other visible door being to the corner property. Iron railings separated the building from the street and protected the lower area. Upstairs in the building were an architect and a firm of "commission agents". Exhibition space was on the ground and lower ground floors. There was electric light, although it must have given an uneven light as Adey said of a somewhat unsatisfactory piece by Conder, "it does not look bad in the darker part of the room". Heating was provided by open fires at the rear of the gallery; above the mantelpiece was another favoured spot for paintings. The small size of the gallery meant that pictures were exhibited in a near domestic setting and this was emphasised by the use of props, including a piano and tables. These, of course, helped when displaying small-scale sculptures such as Ricketts's bronzes or Conder's fans.

Stanley Makower, a contributor to the *Yellow Book* and a possible shareholder in the gallery, described a visit in 1899:

> I cherish my first impression of Ryder Street which, thank Heaven, is to remain undisturbed. I see Robert flitting between the desk and the door, a kind of animated Christ, confusing his soul with the pictures on the wall and afraid to sell, lest he might imperil a reputation of nineteen centuries. I see pretty Mrs Clifton brewing tea in the first floor front drawing-room and smiling at the shareholders who drop in to see 'how Carfax is going'; I see Albert Rutherston, Esq. leap from his tilbury, throw his reins to the groom and sweep the gallery with his critical eye in three minutes. He pauses, murmurs 'Giotto could have done no better', pauses on his way out at a master of the Slade, mutters 'vile pastiche' at the innocent canvas, and then jumps on the box of his tilbury and drives to see Nellie Farren. [5]

First floor in this context must mean the ground floor. Mrs Clifton was Arthur Clifton's first wife, Florence, whom he had married in 1892 and who, on a visit to Goring with Arthur in 1894 had gone boating with Constance Wilde. Arthur and Florence (known as Marjorie) divorced a few years later after Arthur had become infatuated with the painter Madeleine Fiennes-Clinton Knox; he would marry her in 1919.

It is thought that another shareholder in the gallery was Bernard Shaw. It was Shaw who, in 1905, wrote to Ross to introduce a sculptor newly arrived in Britain whose work might suit Carfax, and who was anxious to exhibit there. The sculptor was Jacob Epstein who, said Shaw, thought Carfax "the centre of real art in London".[6] Although he never exhibited at Carfax, Ross would, a few years later, commission him to create the memorial to Oscar Wilde in Père Lachaise cemetery. Epstein claimed that he knew nothing of the commission until after it had been announced at the Ritz dinner for Ross in 1908[7] – presumably another secret Adey kept.

An argument with the always rather irascible Conder over the difference between what the gallery paid him for art and what the public was charged led Conder to accuse Rothenstein of making him sign an unfair contract while drunk. This was clearly not true, but Rothenstein felt "sorely troubled; I must at all costs withdraw from Carfax".[8] When Ross stepped in to take over the business, Rothenstein was relieved from an irksome engagement, while Fothergill, "who had lost neither friends nor capital, was well content with the new arrangement".[9] Ross visited Fothergill in Rome at the end of 1899 and told him of the proposals for the Carfax.

It has not been established where Ross found the money to allow Fothergill to recover his capital. Ross was known to complain of being hard up, although he might have been able to call on family money for the purchase. The timing, however, fits with the possibility of Adey providing the backing. Adey's mother Emma died on 9 April 1900 and it was in the spring of that year that Ross's offer was made. Probate was not granted until September, when Adey was named as sole beneficiary for property valued at £9,428 12s 8d. Much of this was tied up in land and buildings but would still have allowed him to finance the takeover which probably cost a little over £500. If he did, the delay between his mother's death and the granting of probate put him in an awkward position. In a letter of August 1900, Lord Alfred Douglas said,

> I am very sorry, More, that you are so hard up. It is too maddening. I have spent exactly £10,000 since the beginning of February, and so am very hard up myself. Nevertheless I venture to send you a small Xmas present, which I hope you won't mind accepting from a young friend (I was going to say 'an old friend', but that sounds awful!)

The last exhibition under the original management was in April and was of works by Charles Conder, who had quickly lost his antipathy to the gallery.

Rothenstein credited Ross and Clifton with turning Carfax into a proper business, although the fact that Clifton had supposedly been responsible for the "business side" since the gallery's inception rather undermines his role in the transformation. Rothenstein had been critical of Clifton's tight hold on the gallery's finances, but only, it seems, as it applied to Rothenstein's own cash flow problems. Ross was very critical of the efficiency of the gallery staff, and particularly of their record keeping. Rothenstein makes no mention of Adey in any of his volumes of autobiography, but it is clear from the little extant evidence that Adey's meticulous approach must have contributed enormously to the newly reinvigorated Carfax. Adey, Ross and Clifton had of course worked fairly closely together during Wilde's imprisonment and knew each other's methods.

The first exhibition under new management was of "drawings, lithographs and portraits" by Rothenstein in November 1900, followed the next month by "oil paintings and paintings on silk" by Conder and "drawings of Auvergne and Burgundy" by Rothenstein. There were five exhibitions in 1901 and seven in each year until Ross and Adey withdrew at the end of 1908.

In the 1890s Ross and Adey – and sometimes Reggie Turner – had rooms in Hornton Street, a turning off Kensington High Street almost opposite the tube station. Nowadays a highly salubrious and expensive address, but perhaps not quite so desirable then. When Charles Conder returned from Paris in May 1899 he too took rooms in Hornton Street, but instead of staying there, took to slipping in to Rothenstein's house nearby, explaining in a letter to Rothenstein:

> I am very happy here and feel each evening like a great cuckoo when I get into your bed. I hope you don't mind? but my own one in Hornton St is too buggy. Your housekeeper is most charming & attends to my every want.[10]

Considering that Carfax was such an important gallery, responsible for the first or early exhibitions of so many important twentieth century artists, there is very little information about it. The great Sickert expert, Wendy Baron, when she was preparing the Sickert exhibition in 1974, went to see the widow of Arthur Clifton and Mrs Clifton admitted that, as part of her war effort to save fuel, she had burned all the papers relating to Carfax.[11]

It is fortunate that her patriotism extended no further because it was in Clifton's widow's trunk that the notebooks containing the manuscript of Acts I and II of *The Importance of Being Earnest* were found. These are now in the New York Public Library.[12]

Adey was certainly not a sleeping partner; the tact he had shown in the negotiations around Wilde's imprisonment came to the fore in dealings with often difficult artists; he arranged the hanging of shows and talked commercial opportunities with artists and dealers. He dealt with invitations and catalogues and corresponded with the gallery's artists, although little of that correspondence survives.

There are few mentions of Carfax in published recollections and none of those mentions Adey; but there is a letter of December 1901 from Bernard Shaw to Max Beerbohm which may refer to Adey. Shaw had gone to the gallery to see Beerbohm's cartoons and had – "to my horror" – found his wife intent on purchasing "the capitalist G.B.S., with the object of concealing or destroying it as a libel on her husband's charms". Shaw – anthropomorphising the gallery – concludes:

> When my wife demurred to the Capitalist, Carfax suggested, with dealerlike urbanity, that he was sure Mr Beerbohm would accept a commission from her for a special caricature if she would explain the style of thing she preferred. He was profoundly serious.[13]

This certainly sounds more like Adey than Ross.

One series of letters which does survive is to Charles Conder concerning his exhibition of fans in 1902. Conder's previous exhibitions at Carfax had been commercial successes but, for whatever reason, this one in 1902 proved to be a disaster.[14]

Adey's letters to Conder and to Conder's wife Stella Maris show that he was intimately concerned with all aspects of the gallery, going into details of the arrangement of pictures and fans within the space, the issuing of invitations, critical approaches and the pricing of pictures. He also advises on where to get fans made up and has ideas for developing customers. Although Conder's half of the correspondence does not survive, it is clear that while all around found Conder difficult to deal with, not least because of his habit of selling pictures privately and undercutting Carfax, Adey maintained equable relations with him and his wife. There is even an unusual insight into his relationship with Ross, when he says to Conder, "I believe Ross has written to you about French's oil *Souvenir de Chopin*, he gave me the letter to read, but I merely glanced at it, as it seemed to me quite superfluous, so I do not quite know what he said." For all Ross's ability to form close and lasting friendships, he could also be irascible and – as was the case with Douglas in the 1890s – Adey may have been the one to patch things up.

Adey would undoubtedly have overseen the removal, in March 1905, from Ryder Street around the corner to 24 Bury Street. The only description we have been left of those premises is by Paul Nash, writing of his first visit in 1912, after Adey and Ross had withdrawn:

> The Carfax was probably the most distinguished and exclusive gallery in London at that time. ... It was sponsored in some mysterious way by both William Rothenstein and Robert Ross, but its recent success was largely due to its manager, Arthur Clifton, who originally acted merely as legal adviser.
>
> The gallery was situated in one of those expensive, rather secret streets running between Piccadilly and St James's. It consisted of one exhibition room only, which was at the back. There was a spacious shop-window and a narrow passage leading into the gallery proper. On the left side of this annexe was the opening of a spiral staircase down to the basement, storeroom and office. Beyond this aperture the room had the benefit of its full width, but was hampered by an immense 'Old Master', of impressive but dubious design, which hung on the opposite wall. Between this and the street door was what remained of the right-hand wall, an open space interrupted here and there by odd drawings, and small paintings.

Nash also gives a rare description of Arthur Clifton:

> A B Clifton was a big man rather inclined to be stout. He was eminently flatfooted, but always conveyed a dignified presence crowned by a rather distinguished head.

Clifton was a lawyer and Nash's descriptions suggest he carried a courtroom demeanour into the gallery:

> Clifton always kept his sense of humour just on the other side of his pose of melancholy, like the sun round the corner of a cloud.

But it was a pose; when "tickled" by a joke, "His heavy-lidded eyes rolled slightly and a wholly charming smile slowly traversed his face".[15]

Nash's exhibition was not "in the gallery room proper for that is booked years ahead but on the wall as you go in". He still managed to exhibit twenty drawings on that wall; Gordon Bottomley remembered that first show, "when Carfax's paid you with golden sovereigns, and you and Jack made patterns on the carpet with them".[16] Maxwell Armfield was on show in the "gallery proper".

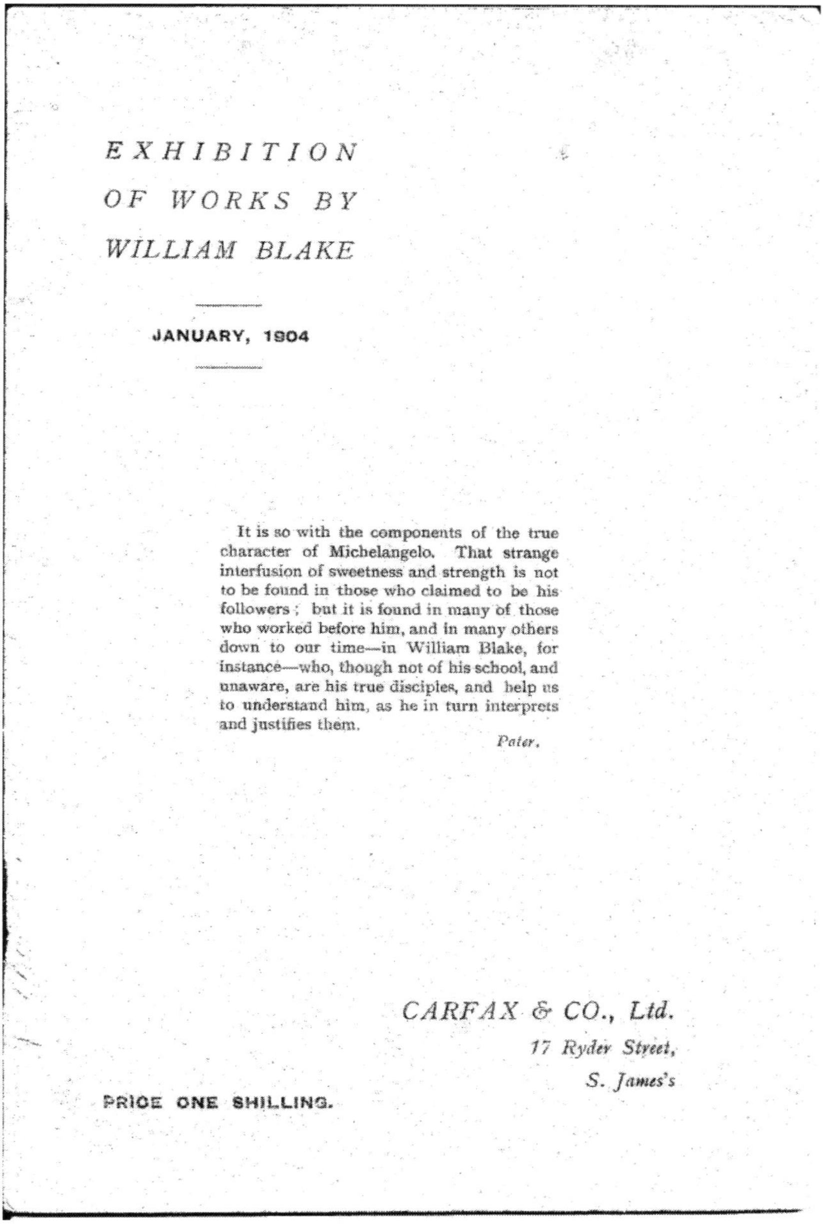

EXHIBITION

OF WORKS BY

WILLIAM BLAKE

JANUARY, 1904

It is so with the components of the true character of Michelangelo. That strange interfusion of sweetness and strength is not to be found in those who claimed to be his followers; but it is found in many of those who worked before him, and in many others down to our time—in William Blake, for instance—who, though not of his school, and unaware, are his true disciples, and help us to understand him, as he in turn interprets and justifies them.

Pater.

CARFAX & CO., Ltd.

17 Ryder Street,

S. James's

PRICE ONE SHILLING.

Fig. 3 Catalogue of the Carfax Gallery's William Blake exhibition, 1904.

The move to Bury Street was marked with an important exhibition

> The new Carfax Gallery in Bury-street will be most interestingly inaugurated this month by an exhibition of sketches by Mr Sargent. Messrs Carfax stand alone in having induced the gifted Anglo-American to let such things leave his studio for exhibition purposes.[17]

The rooms were no bigger than they had been in Ryder Street, variously described as a "charming new gallery" and "no more delightful little room in London". The *London Daily News* at the end of March gave a glowing review of the Sargent exhibition, spoiled only by a headline which referred to the "New Fairfax Gallery".

Exhibitions were widely noted in the press and several garnered long and complimentary reviews. The *London Daily News*, in its review of the art world in 1904 by Frank Rinder said:

> No more memorable exhibition was held than that, early in the year, at the Carfax Gallery, of works by William Blake. At the same gallery in Ryder-street we have had the greatly exhilarating

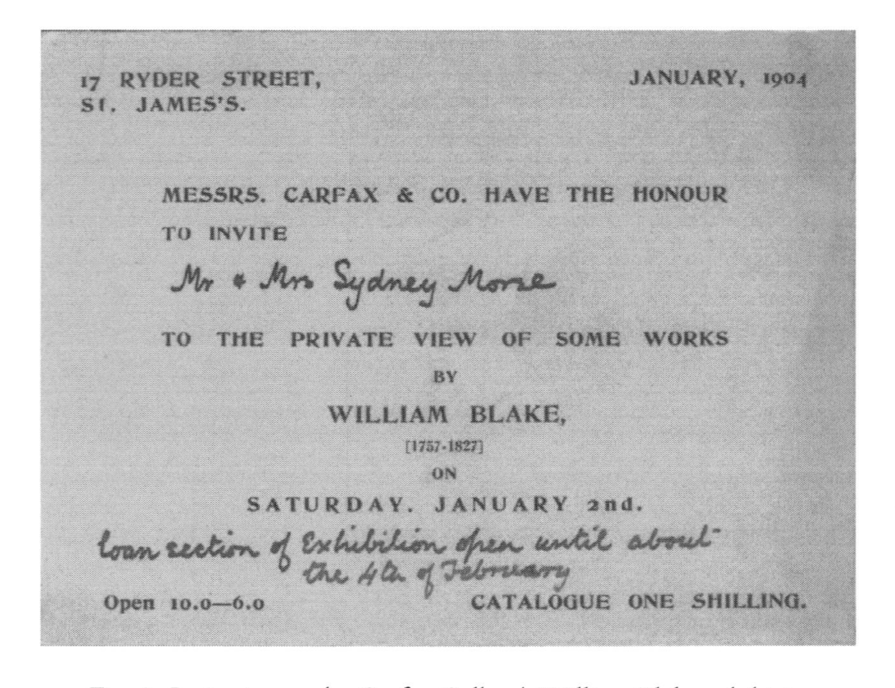

17 RYDER STREET, ST. JAMES'S. JANUARY, 1904

MESSRS. CARFAX & CO. HAVE THE HONOUR TO INVITE

Mr & Mrs Sydney Morse

TO THE PRIVATE VIEW OF SOME WORKS BY WILLIAM BLAKE, [1757-1827] ON SATURDAY. JANUARY 2nd.

loan section of Exhibition open until about the 4th of February

Open 10.0—6.0 CATALOGUE ONE SHILLING.

Fig. 4 Invitation to the Carfax Gallery's William Blake exhibition, annotated by More Adey.

> witticisms of Mr Max Beerbohm, the exquisite, if "evil" pen drawings of Aubrey Beardsley – three or four of them acquired for South Kensington – works by the follower of Blake, Edward Calvert. Nor must there be forgotten the Coronation picture of Mr Abbey, destined for the collection of the King when it has made a round of the Colonies, and Whistler's Peacock Room, now in the possession of Mr Charles L Frere, Detroit.[18]

Blake and Beerbohm were particular Carfax favourites. In 1901 they exhibited around one hundred Beerbohm cartoons and over fifty in 1908. The Blake exhibition of 1904 was considered ground breaking and reviewers commented that it proved Blake was not just for the elite. Above the fireplace in the gallery hung *Elohim creating Adam*, which was on loan from the collection formed by Blake's friend Thomas Butts. According to one review it was at this exhibition that "M Rodin first made the acquaintance of the artist's work, and was greatly struck by it". Two years later the gallery held another Blake exhibition, when it was reported that an "entire collection of pictures by Blake . ... formed by his friend Butts, has been purchased by the firm". This was an unusual investment for Carfax, but it allowed them to sell *Elohim creating Adam* to Ross and Adey's friend W Graham Robertson. He bequeathed the picture to the Tate Gallery in 1939. The press said of this exhibition:

> Londoners have seldom the advantage of access to so many highly important exhibitions as at the present moment. Immediately to be disengaged from all others, however, is that at the Carfax Gallery, Bury-street, which consists of about 100 works by William Blake.[19]

Carfax was not above some publicity seeking activity. In December 1903 it was widely reported that:

> At the Carfax Gallery yesterday there was to be seen Mr William Strang's portrait of Mr Chamberlain, executed, it is said, between about eleven and twelve o'clock on Tuesday.

The portrait was shown for one afternoon only before being shipped to its purchaser in America. Only critics were invited to the showing, but large numbers of the public viewed it as well. Then, in November 1905, the *London Daily News* carried the headline:

"INSIDERS" AND "OUTSIDERS"

CARFAX v AGNEW

The conservative gallery, Agnew's, had decided, contrary to their normal policy, to stage an exhibition of artists considered "outsiders", that is members of non-Royal Academy bodies like the New English Art Club. These were the sort of artists normally supported by Carfax, but Agnew's had bought the pictures outright to demonstrate their confidence – something Carfax rarely did. Also going against type,

> The little Carfax Gallery, on the other hand – despite the fact that here only has Mr Sargent been induced to hold one-man shows – has been associated with "outsiders," from William Blake, who cordially hated Reynolds, to Aubrey Beardsley, from the vehement Mr A E John to scholarly Mr Fry. But the directors of the Carfax have arranged a show of cabinet pictures by "insiders" to synchronise with the dissimilar venture in Bond-street.
>
> We learn that Sir Edward Poynter will contribute a specially-painted picture, that veterans like Mr Frith and Mr Sant will send, the former a recently-executed version of "Dr Johnson and Mrs Siddons," and that there will be represented amongst others Sir William Richmond, Mr Sargent, whose work will not be for sale, however, Mr Alfred Parsons, Mr J W North, Mr Gow, Mr Tuke, Mr Frank Bramley, Mr Leader, Sir L Alma-Tadema, perhaps Mr Solomon, Mr David Murray, and "moderns" like Mr Brangwyn, Mr Clausen and Mr East.[20]

Alongside the well-known names of the time, there is at least one example of possible family connections. In December 1905 were exhibited some "tinted drawings" of ancient buildings – not the usual Carfax fare – by Arthur Ponsonby, the Liberal candidate for Taunton. Ponsonby was among Adey's family names, and the artist was, like Adey, a west-country man.

But for all the wonderful exhibitions the gallery was not a commercial success. When it was founded, Walter Sickert had high hopes that it would "put out all the other damned fools" and had claimed that "Business is a science. The London dealers have not mastered it". But as the *Guardian* obituary of Arthur Clifton put it in 1932:

> It seemed a gallery run by dilettanti for dilettanti. Somehow it was always afternoon there, and there were always tall, vague, well dressed men talking about unknown poets. Upstairs in a sort of loft were stocks of Aubrey Beardsley drawings and a rare Blake painting on copper, and so it was whispered, some wonderful Botticellis in the very Chianti bottles in which they were smuggled from Italy.[21]

As might be expected, when Ross left Carfax in 1908 to become art critic of the *Morning Post* Adey went as well.

On 18 October 1908 Adey's youngest sister, Emma Elizabeth, wife of Ponsonby Sullivan, died in Folkestone. Her mother, also Emma Elizabeth, had died in 1900, so the deaths of the two women closest to Adey had bracketed his time at the Carfax. The following year, Ponsonby Sullivan became vicar of Rangeworthy, Gloucestershire, near Wotton under Edge.

Clifton remained in charge of the Carfax, and although the exhibitions seemed to become less frequent only a few years after Adey's departure, the gallery remained in existence until January 1932 when, at an Extraordinary General Meeting of the Members, it was resolved to wind up the business voluntarily. Clifton, who was Chairman of the company, and at whose home the meeting was held, was appointed liquidator. The names of the other members were not recorded.

Notes

1 *Men and Memories: Reflections of William Rothenstein 1872-1900*, Faber & Faber, 1931, p. 343

2 Quoted in *Walter Sickert: A Life*, Matthew Sturgis, Harper Collins 2005, p. 267

3 *Glasgow Herald*, 25 January 1900

4 *The Survey of London, Vol XXIX: The Parish of St James Westminster Part One: South of Piccadilly*, Athlone Press 1960, p. 318

5 *William Rothenstein: The Portrait of an Artist in his Time*, Robert Speaight, Eyre and Spottiswoode 1962, p. 144

6 *Bernard Shaw: Collected Letters 1898-1910*, edited by Dan H Laurence, Max Reinhardt 1972, p. 521

7 *Let There Be Sculpture*, Jacob Epstein, Michael Joseph 1940, p. 65

8 A fascinating insight into the early days of the Carfax Gallery is provided by Samuel Shaw in 'The New Ideal Shop: Founding the Carfax Gallery, c1898-1902' in *The British Art Journal*, Vol XIII, No 2, Autumn 2012.

9 Speaight, p. 145

10 Quoted in Speaight, p. 124

11 Letter to the author from the Fine Art Society, 8 February 2002

12 https://www.nypl.org/blog/2016/02/09/trivial-blog-post-serious-people

13 ed. Reinhardt, op cit, p. 248

14 The circumstances surrounding this exhibition, based largely on these letters from Adey, have been described in 'New documents regarding the

Carfax Gallery', Barbara Pezzini, in *The British Art Journal,* Vol XIII, No 2, Autumn 2012.

15 *Outline,* Paul Nash, Faber and Faber 1949, p. 124 et seq

16 *Poet and Painter: Being the Correspondence Between Gordon Bottomley and Paul Nash 1910-1946,* edited by Claude Colleer Abbott and Anthony Bertram, Oxford University Press, 1955, p. 213

17 *London Daily News,* 4 March 1905

18 *London Daily News,* 28 December 1904. Edwin Austin Abbey's picture, "The Coronation of King Edward VII" was painted at his studio in Tite Street – see *The Street of Wonderful Possibilities,* Devon Cox, Frances Lincoln 2015, p. 192 et seq

19 *London Daily News,* 20 June 1906

20 *London Daily News,* 30 November 1905

21 *Manchester Guardian* 8 October 1932

7. THE BURLINGTON MAGAZINE

The *Burlington Magazine* had been founded in 1903 and had already seen its share of editorial and financial problems. The first editor, Robert Dell, left and Charles Holmes, future director of the National Portrait Gallery, took over. Financial support was precarious and Roger Fry – one of the prime movers in the establishment of the magazine and a member of the Consultative Committee – and Holmes steered it to relative security in the years before Adey arrived.[1]

Ross was already a contributor to the *Burlington*; the Carfax advertised in its pages and its exhibitions were reviewed there. Adey's first inclusion in the list of contributors was in October 1908, although his contribution is not identifiable; he then appears as a contributor in every issue until November 1910, by which time he is listed as Assistant Editor – a temporary position "in the absence of Harold Child". Child had been editor of *The Academy* and, at Ross's suggestion, had taken on Alfred Douglas as his assistant before the magazine was sold and Child stepped down. By 1908 he was heavily involved with the *Times Literary Supplement* and the *Times*, as well as producing his own slim volumes. When and for how long he held a position at the *Burlington*, and why "the absence" is unclear.

In April 1913 Adey's erstwhile brother in law, Ponsonby Sullivan, who by now was Diocesan Inspector of Schools for the Bishop of Gloucester as well as vicar of Rangeworthy, married again. His bride was another girl from Wotton under Edge, Muriel Helen Forty. Neither Adey nor Ross is listed among the guests at the wedding, so it appears that this long-standing friendship may have come to an end.

Quite how Adey made the transition from the Carfax to the *Burlington* is not known, although he and Ross had enough friends in the worlds of art history and criticism to engineer such a position. From January 1914 to May 1919 Adey was listed as Co-Editor alongside Roger Fry and Lionel Cust. Cust and Holmes had effectively exchanged jobs: Cust had been Director of the National Portrait Gallery but his eyesight was failing and – much, apparently to his own surprise – Holmes was appointed to succeed him. Cust, while retaining his role as Surveyor of Pictures in Ordinary to His Majesty, moved to the *Burlington*. Holmes wrote an apologetic farewell in his editor's notes:

> Acceptance of an official post compels a change in the position of the senior editor of The Burlington Magazine. It is clear that in these columns he cannot henceforth review the conduct either of

the Government which employs him or of his future colleagues with the complete independence proper to the position which he has held hitherto. Thus while he may continue to watch the interests of the magazine, the responsibility for the editorship will, he trusts, be now transferred to far more distinguished hands, in whose care such reputation as the magazine possesses cannot fail to be enhanced.[2]

Although Holmes had to step down from his formal positions with the magazine, he notes in his autobiography that

> What gratified me particularly was the almost universal wish that I should not give up the 'Burlington'. Our efforts to establish a sort of nucleus of practical sense in administration and of tolerance in criticism, had not, apparently, failed.[3]

Despite what Wilde said about his practical abilities, these qualities would have appealed to Adey. Adey and Cust could not have been more different. Lionel Cust was the Eton educated son of a knight; his mother was the daughter of the Earl of Darnley. In 1895 he had married Sybil, daughter of Baron Lyttleton and the niece of Mrs Gladstone. In one of her letters, Sybil summed up their relationship

> She gathers at her table
> The highest in the land;
> How one so young keeps house so well
> They fail to understand.
>
> And while her daily tasks at home
> Rejoice her modest heart,
> Her husband a great name has made
> In the history of Art.[4]

They lived in Windsor and were comfortable surrounded by royalty; as Sybil notes after one evening of "brilliant entertainment" and "sparkling dialogue in his native tongue between Graf Metternich, the German Ambassador and The Hon. Mrs Cust at table", "Princesses vied for Lionel's company after dinner". This is not a world in which Adey would have been comfortable.[5]

His time at the magazine and his uneasy relationship with Roger Fry have been well documented by Barbara Pezzini, who described the difference between the writing styles of the two men:

> ... where Fry is discursive, populist, charming, subjective and full of confidence, Adey is historicist, attentive to detail and bordering on the pedantic.[6]

In Adey's case, "bordering" seems a mild description, but his style was important for much of what the *Burlington* stood for:

> Adey's writings for the Burlington are an interesting alternative to Fry's more formalist essays, as they attempt to establish a style of art criticism that integrates formal analysis with archival and iconographical research.[7]

During his time as editor Adey contributed a number of notes and reviews of exhibitions and catalogues as well as three obituaries, but only four full articles: 'Miniatures Ascribed to Sultan Muhammad' in June 1914, 'Records of Various Works of Art in Belgium (The Lierre triptych)' in November of the same year, 'William Blake's "Nelson"' in January 1915 and 'An Icon Illustrating a Greek Hymn' in February 1919. Ross also contributed pieces on William Blake, including one in 1906 when the Carfax was holding its second Blake exhibition. Adey had taken a particular interest in Blake at Carfax, with the following acknowledgment of his expertise in Basil de Selincourt's biography of the artist:

> Mr. More Adey furthered my studies by placing his wide and accurate knowledge of Blake's technical processes completely at my disposal, and did me most generous service in assisting me to procure adequate illustration for the work.[8]

There was increasing divergence between the views of Adey and Roger Fry both as to the conduct of art historical research and the promotion of modern artists. Fry was moving ever closer to the Post-Impressionists, while Adey favoured artists he had known and exhibited at Carfax and members of the New English Art Club; for all his European taste in literature, Adey remained English in his taste for paintings. Even near the beginning of Adey's time on the magazine the atmosphere cannot have been pleasant; in 1910 Fry's exhibition "Manet and the Post-Impressionists" – an exhibition for which Cust joined Fry on the Executive Committee – was denounced in no uncertain terms in the *Morning Post* by Adey's friend Charles Ricketts. Robert Ross was the art critic of the *Morning Post* so, as with the relationship with Douglas, Adey was caught between opposing parties.

Fry's influence was strong and the editors bowed to the inevitable, whatever their personal leanings (although Cust seems to have stayed outside this argument to some extent, perhaps because his tastes were not for the modern either English or European). In spring 1917 Fry wrote to a contributor that "We must absolutely bring in new material. Now I am trying to introduce articles on Modern art – serious art of course". At the end of the following year he was talking of serious reform at the magazine, reorganising staff and "becoming a wire pulling, intriguing politician". By March 1919 Cust and Adey had both turned sixty and were seen as a barrier to Fry's ambitions for the magazine; Fry wrote to Vanessa Bell:

> There are awful rows about the Burlington and a general atmosphere of hatred and fury against me among the cultured. ... We are really getting the wretched paper in hand.[9]

Neither of the major biographies of Roger Fry mentions Adey, and his published letters contain only one reference, including Adey in a list of donors for a proposed – but never built – memorial to Renoir.

Working with Adey for part of this time was Christopher Millard, whose relationship with Adey would extend well into his retirement to Wotton under Edge. Millard may have started working there as early as 1906 after he was released from prison,[10] but that looks unlikely as although Ross may have got him the job, it would probably have needed Adey there to smooth the way. He was certainly there in 1911 when he complained of being "rather rushed about" at the magazine, and a piece appeared that summer over his initials. By April 1913, however, he wrote to Walter Ledger that he had "chucked" the *Burlington* "so you can call any afternoon in the week".[11]

In 1914 Millard lost his other employment as secretary to Robert Ross. This was because Ross had become concerned that Millard was not to be relied upon in the continuing battle with Douglas. There had been attempts by Douglas to bribe Millard to make damaging statements about Ross following the collapse of Douglas's attempts to get Ross prosecuted on the "evidence" of Millard's lover, Charley Garratt. The police had dismissed Garratt's statement about being seduced by Ross on the basis that he was known to be unreliable, and Garratt later claimed never to have met Ross. Millard was without income and Adey was able – just – to offer him some money. There was talk of £2 but Adey could only manage £1 "until I know how my balance stands". Adey always seems to have been pressed for money.

For three weeks in early 1917 Adey is listed as resident at the Grand Pump Room Hotel in Bath. In March Ross wrote to Carlos Blacker to say he had been staying with Adey in Bath for a few days and that Adey was taking the waters for his sciatica.

Adey's name appeared for the last time as a co-editor in May 1919 and he effectively retired to Wotton under Edge. Six lines in *The Times* of 14 July announced:

> Mr Lionel Cust, C.V.O., and Mr More Adey have severed their connection with the Burlington Magazine Company (Limited). Mr Lionel Cust having ceased to be a managing director of the company, and Mr Lionel Cust and Mr More Adey having ceased to be editors of the *Burlington Magazine*.

The following January he wrote to D S MacColl explaining why Fry had not commented in the *Burlington* on MacColl's articles:

> The well known fact that Cust and I both left the Magazine – not on account of 'Omegaismus', but of 'Fryismus' would disincline him from appearing very prominently in the Magazine.[12]

Quite what difference Adey saw between Omegaismus and Fryismus is unclear as Fry was deeply involved in the Omega Workshops. Fry also left the *Burlington* in 1919, although he remained as a director; one influential enough to persuade the Board to appoint his choice of editor – Robert Rattray Tatlock. Tatlock would remain as editor until 1933, one year before Fry's death.

The Carfax and the *Burlington* provided the only periods of paid employment in Adey's life.

Notes

1 The early history of the *Burlington Magazine* has been taken largely from two articles: 'A more and more important work': Roger Fry and The Burlington Magazine, Caroline Elam, *The Burlington Magazine*, Vol CXLV, No 1200, March 2003, and More Adey, the Carfax Gallery and 'The Burlington Magazine', Barbara Pezzini, *The Burlington Magazine*, Vol CLIII, No 1305, December 2011

2 *The Burlington Magazine*, No 79, Vol XVI, October 1909

3 *Self and Partners (Mostly Self)*, C J Holmes, Constable, 1936, p. 262

4 *The Letters of Sybil Cust*, edited by Sarah Bailey, p. 104d

5 *Ibid*, p. 147

6 Pezzini, op cit p. 812

7 Pezzini, op cit p. 806

8 *William Blake*, Basil de Selincourt, Duckworth 1909, p. v

9 *The Letters of Roger Fry* Vol 2, edited by Denys Sutton, Chatto and Windus, 1972, p. 448

10 *Yours Loyally: A Life of Christopher Sclater Millard*, Maria Roberts, FeedARead.com Publishing, 2014. Roberts claims that Millard started at *The*

Burlington almost immediately after his release from Oxford Prison in late summer 1906 (p.76), but she says that Cust and Adey were the editors at that time although they did not become editors until much later.

11 Millard to Ledger 1 April 1913, University College Oxford

12 Quoted in Pezzini, op cit p. 814

8. THE DEATH OF ROBERT ROSS

Although he was working throughout the war, it must have affected Adey deeply. Ross who was then living in Half Moon Street writes about the Zeppelin raids and the "dust bomb" which fell on the house next door (which would have killed the lady of the house had she not been in someone else's bed at the time). Pip Blacker, the son of Ross and Adey's friend Carlos, was awarded the Military Cross and visited them while on leave. There is a letter from Ross to Carlos Blacker in which Ross says:

> I do hope dear Pip will be allowed leave shortly. He will tell you about my unhappy nephew who came to terrible grief. Pip stood by him so splendidly. He has had to leave the Guards & will enlist as a private in some regiment but you had better pretend to know nothing till you see Pip.[1]

The nephew in question was Cecil Sprigge, the son of Samuel Squire Sprigge and Ross's nephew by marriage.

Another letter from Cecil to Carlos Blacker tells him what a wonderful friend Pip has been and how Cecil knows the life he leads makes him unworthy of Pip's friendship. He then re-enlisted as an able seaman – a phrase Ross puts in quotes![2]

Cecil had been hoping to contribute to the first number of Edith Sitwell's *Wheels*, but told her brother Sacheverell that he would not do so because he was caught up in a "painful cause celebre". "I am paying the penalty for 'seeing red' on one unfortunate occasion ... I hope you will think of me in charity, & excuse in your heart the vulgarity of my being discovered in an over-literal discipleship of Plato". As Sacheverell Sitwell's biographer has said, Cecil's father "should have been understanding; instead he sent Cecil to a private 'nervous hospital'".[3] It seems likely to have been the same one to which Sprigge was to commit Adey a few years later. Blacker's younger son Robin was killed in 1915 at the age of eighteen and Ross travelled to Torquay to comfort Carlos Blacker.

It is to the meetings of poets and others in Half Moon Street that we owe the one lengthy description we have of More Adey. In *Noble Essences*, the fifth volume of his memoirs, Osbert Sitwell says of Adey:

> "By origin a squire from Gloucestershire, he had played some part in the literary life of the 'nineties, and had latterly been for several years Editor of the *Burlington Magazine*. I greatly liked this intensely fantastic character. In appearance, at the time I met him, he resembled, I see now, a water-colour drawing of

Lenin as he would have been rendered through the etherealised vision and by the etiolative hand of Burne-Jones: a small figure, with a bearded face of pale complexion and minutely lined. How much he knew of art I shall never be aware, for he scarcely ever mentioned a picture in front of me, but talked always of war and politics. In politics, he took, as the misleading phrase goes, an advanced view, and though thoroughly innocuous, so kind that he would not injure even someone he much disliked, and so ineffective as to be incapable of hunting a midge, it pleased him to dramatise himself to himself as a dangerous anarchist. In this imposture he was entirely successful. I remember his taking me round to show me some new rooms he had found – or rather, that others had been obliged to find for him, - on the ground floor of a house in Burlington Gardens, and his remarking to me in all seriousness, pointing in the direction of the street:

'This place has great advantages. It's convenient for the police. Whenever they want to know where I am, they can just send someone round the corner from Vine Street to look through the window. It saves us all a lot of trouble.'

When I first met him, I recollect he was absorbed in framing a question that he was intent on persuading a friend, who was a member of Parliament, to ask in the House of Commons. More was very anti-war in his attitude, and also resented being unable to go abroad. The question he had designed was to be addressed to the Secretary of State for the Home Department, and ran: "Can a British subject voluntarily denaturalise himself, and be then in consequence compulsorily deported?"

Though Robbie was intensely sociable, and so frequently in More Adey's company, More often used to make him irritable: for example, he never knew what time it was, and after working late at the office of the *Burlington*, would arrive round at 40 Half Moon Street at two AM thinking it was seven PM and sit there, expecting to be taken out to dinner. Though Robbie liked sitting up late, he did not like sitting up as late as that, but it would be impossible to move More without hurting his feelings. ... More Adey was also persuaded in his own mind that Gold Flake cigarettes – in those days cheap as postage stamps, and more easily procurable – could only be obtained through the good offices of poor Miss Burton (Ross's housekeeper), to whom he would repair in shopping hours or whom he would rouse at night, begging her to secure a packet for him – though if the shops were open, all he had to do was to go to the tobacconist next door and buy one.[4]

The reference to Burlington Gardens is interesting, because either Sitwell is mistaken or Adey was at that address for a very short time. In summer 1919 Adey wrote to his cousin Capel Adye from his rooms at 22 Old Burlington Street – only a few doors away from the magazine's offices – to say that "these rooms are so expensive for what I get that I must move as soon as I can".[5]

The idea of Adey attracting the attention of the police is unlikely, except in the context of Douglas's witch hunt against homosexuals, particularly Ross. Douglas appears never to have made any allegations involving Adey, so Sitwell can only be reflecting a fantasy on Adey's part.

Another of Ross's guests at this time was Wilfred Owen, who wrote in 1917 to his mother, saying:

> I've been busy this evening with my terrific poem (at present) called "The Deranged". (Now called "Mental Cases") This poem the Editor of the *Burlington Magazine* .... old More Adey, I say, solemnly prohibited me from sending to the English Review, on the grounds that "the English Review should not be encouraged!!![6]

What Adey had against the *English Review* may indicate his own reticence in some areas. At this time the *English Review* was owned and edited by Austin Harrison who had not only increased circulation and made the magazine profitable, but had taken it in a less conservative editorial direction, with a new attitude in particular to sexual matters. Adey would probably have been sympathetic to the magazine's political stance in the period immediately before the war when it warned of impending danger, but he may have been out of tune with some of the less traditional literary contributors which included Aldous Huxley and Katherine Mansfield. Owen's description of "old More Adey" (he was 59 in 1917) and the solemnity of Adey's prohibition reinforce the picture given by Sitwell.

Similarly, Siegfried Sassoon remembered that his poem "They" was "written at 40 Half Moon Street about 1am after a long evening with Robbie Ross, More Adey and Roderick Meiklejohn. I was so sleepy I could hardly keep my eyes open, but the thing just wrote itself."[7] This was in October 1916. Meiklejohn might look a little out of place in this company, being a civil servant and economist; but he was a friend of Sassoon's, a fellow member of the Reform Club with Ross and was to serve on the committee of The Contemporary Art Society. He also appears to have had rooms in Half Moon Street around this time.

It is from the death of Robert Ross in 1918 that Adey's final decline can be dated. They had been together for around thirty years and although they led separate lives they were forever being linked as Ross and Adey.

Nobody of his acquaintance has recorded seeing him in London again, nor did he take advantage of the end of the war to travel abroad. He had spent a great deal of time at home in Wotton in the early years of the century, so leaving London cannot have been a wrench. Small town life clearly appealed and he had regularly taken part in the local flower and produce shows, being highly placed in more than one category. In 1906 he was among those listed as having had most success in the amateur classes at the Wotton under Edge Carnival which, as well as flower and produce competitions, fireworks, a procession with bands and a "trade advertisement class", featured a number of "old English sports" including a "greasy pig contest for women" in which "Mrs Underhill secured the porker after a short scrabble". The high point for Adey was in 1913 when he took first prize and a silver medal in the "cut flowers arranged for effect" class.

Adey wrote to Cecil Sprigge following Ross's death a letter which looks even sadder in view of events seven years later:

> I am ten years older than dear Robbie and his vitality of mind and of resistance – especially – had in 30 years' close and devoted friendship communicated itself to me, and had prevented me from enclosing myself within a wall of impenetrable reserve. I see that effect of Robbie in everyone who knew him, as well as the strong feelings of affection which he inspired in all sorts and kinds of minds, even when he was opposed to them as with great acumen over business matters! ... it struck me when I saw him about one and a half hours after death that he could not have suffered in articulo mortis, there was no sign of any struggle. That is some comfort. I never have been able to make out why, but suffering by Robbie has always seemed to me more poignant to see than in anyone else. It is also a blessing that he had not started for Australia; I always hated the idea of his going ... No one can ever be to you what Robbie has been, no one can ever be to me what he has been, but I should like to make up to you, dear Cecil, whatever little I can of the loss, and you can always count on me as long as I live.[8]

Ross's will had been written before the war, and Adey was not mentioned. His brother Alec and his two nieces were the executors and, with the exception of his Wilde manuscripts, letters and copyrights which he had left to Cyril and Vyvyan Holland, and two pictures destined for the British Museum, the entire estate was left to the executors. However, immediately before his death Ross had been planning to go to Australia and had drawn up a new will. The major change was necessitated by the death of Cyril Holland in 1915 but, according to Maureen Borland, he "had long been concerned that, should he die, a number of his closest friends would be impoverished, and he planned to set up a trust fund". Borland's conversations with one of the proposed trustees discovered that Adey was to be the main beneficiary. As his housekeeper Nellie Burton was to receive an annuity of £100, and Millard, Sprigge and Alfred Lambart each to receive £50 a year, we must assume that Adey was to receive more than £100 a year. The new will was never signed and Alec Ross could only submit the original will for probate.

Alec Ross clearly did not exclude Adey; in September 1922 Adey wrote to Osbert Burdett returning some things he had come across "among Robert Ross's papers". At this point he was staying at the Curzon Hotel in London but was leaving town shortly after writing. He told Burdett that, should Ross have had anything else belonging to Burdett he should notify Alec Ross and in any case he should send Alec an acknowledgment "as I send them during his absence".

As with so much else in, and after, Robert Ross's life, it was left to his brother to sort things out. It is probable that he carried out Ross's wishes in at least some respects, with Adey becoming Wilde's literary executor even though this was not mentioned in the original will.

Notes

1 Ross to Blacker 1 October 1916. Private collection

2 Ross to Blacker 12 December 1916. Private collection

3 *Sacheverell Sitwell: Splendours and Miseries* by Sarah Bradford, Sinclair-Stevenson, 1993, p. 71

4 *Noble Essences*, Osbert Sitwell, Macmillan 1950, p. 102

5 Adey and Capel were corresponding about family history, but with only one side of the correspondence extant, little can be gleaned from it.

6 Sitwell, op cit, p. 98

7 *Siegfried's Journey*, Siegfried Sassoon, Faber 1945, p. 35

8 Quoted in *Wilde's Devoted Friend: a Life of Robert Ross 1869-1918*, Maureen Borland, Lennard Publishing 1990, p. 287

9. LAST YEARS

One day – probably in 1925 – Vyvyan Holland went to Wotton-under-Edge to visit Adey. There he took the photographs which are the only known portraits of the adult Adey and therefore the way he has been remembered. Vyvyan Holland had only met Robert Ross for the first time in late 1907 at the instigation of Mrs Carew. Three months later Ross organised a dinner party in celebration of Vyvyan's 21st birthday; the dinner was at Ross and Adey's house in Vicarage Gardens in Kensington and it may have been here that Vyvyan first met Adey. Apart from Ross, Adey and Holland the guests were Sir William Richmond, Ricketts and Shannon, Henry James, Reggie Turner, William Rothenstein, Ronald Firbank, Sir Coleridge Kennard and Cyril Holland.

Adey was then present at the dinner at the Ritz in December 1908 to celebrate the publication of Wilde's *Collected Works*. It was a glittering and over-subscribed occasion which assembled a lot of old friends. Adey was seated between Ada Leverson and the historian and later novelist John Pollock. Reggie Turner was the other side of Pollock and Stewart Headlam was opposite Ada. A press photograph of the event shows Adey looking rather like King George V, with a well-trimmed naval style "full set" of beard and moustache.[1]

In 1921 the Beaumont Press published the first of two volumes of Wilde's letters to Ross called *After Reading*. Ross had worked with Millard before the First World War to prepare this volume and Ross had written an introduction which was not used. After the war Adey also wrote an introduction, again not used and, finally, the book appeared with a short preface, presumably by Millard. The following year a companion volume – *After Berneval* – was published, this time with an introduction by Adey. Millard and Adey were already close from their working relationship at the *Burlington* but both he and Holland seem to have become frustrated by Adey's approach which was typically both careful and dilatory. Vyvyan Holland at one point said to Millard that while he wanted to give Adey the opportunity to criticise the Notes for *After Berneval*, "We need not, of course, take his suggestions!" He also gave Adey an ultimatum that unless he sent his introduction in a week, "we will write our own".

Millard arranged for the American publisher Reynolds to issue editions of both books, strictly limited to 23 copies each. Adey's introduction to *After Berneval* was longer in this edition and the editing of the letters was less severe. When the booksellers Dulau & Co issued a catalogue of Wilde

Fig. 5 Photographs of More Adey taken in 1925 by Vyvyan Holland in the garden of Under-the-Hill House. The third photograph in the group is reproduced on the cover

material in 1928, it included the American editions of both books together with the unedited typescript of 130 letters from Wilde to Ross, many of which were not in the books. The catalogue says:

> Those who possess Beaumont's two volumes have merely the vaguest outline of a part of the story, and no clue is supplied to them which would assist them to fill in this bare outline. The few who own or have seen a copy of Reynolds' edition are a little more at home with this part of the tale, but no one who has not read the whole of these letters as they stand in this typescript is capable of forming a full and complete judgment of the position. The letters are full in detail and frank in statement, and as they were all written to Robert Ross, a friend from whom Wilde had neither the wish nor the motive to conceal his true attitude towards things, it is only in these letters that one can appreciate what the position was and for what attitude to life he really stood.

Adey's introduction for the American edition was reduced for Beaumont's edition and notes Adey had given to Millard about the Wilde letters, including identifying individuals mentioned in them were discarded by Millard. Apart from minor editorial changes, the following, which constitutes the main omission from the American edition shows Adey's depth of feeling, as well as the prose style which was irritating Millard and Holland. Expressing surprise at the popularity of *After Reading* because the subjects of the letters in it were "intimate and trivial", he continued:

> It is only in the present volume that this matter of public interest is discussed. However moralizers who confuse the spheres of art and ethics may regret the fact, the appeal of that highly personal volume shows that Oscar Wilde's mere personality has an attraction for the clearer-eyed in all countries of the world where the Humanities hold their "absolute values." He continues to attract them, himself, apart from his literary production, for the very reason that "the Nemesis of circumstances, the Nemesis of character" was "too strong" for him and rendered his course of life in his decline as he thought, a "problem for which there is no solution."
>
> That I was particularly cognisant of many incidents referred to in the present volume is evident from the text; at any rate, my friendship with the dead as with their living representatives imperatively prevents me from withholding this otherwise quite superfluous preface to letters which cry aloud from deep to deep of the human intelligence.

The following year, in response to praise for the book from Osbert Burdett, Adey wrote:

> As regards the prefatorial note signed by me; I was extremely reluctant to write it, and only did so in compelling circumstances, too long & not interesting enough for me to trouble you with now. I made a stringent condition that it should be "passed" by Alec Ross, but I do not know whether he liked the precise form in which it finally appeared. As in all three-cornered correspondences we got tired of the subject.[2]

Adey was also corresponding with Millard at this time about books, presumably destined for Millard's book-dealing business, including issues of the *Spirit Lamp*, which Adey said he could supply. They were also assembling a list of Ross's literary output and Adey told Millard he would put his name forward to Alec Ross to compile a Ross bibliography (which did not materialise).

Although there must have been subsequent contact between Vyvyan Holland and Adey, there is no evidence of any until the trip to Wotton when the photographs were taken. In 1935 Vyvyan wrote to Reggie Turner a letter mainly devoted to the topic of A J A Symons, but there is a short reference to Adey which is the only comment we have on his incarceration:

> "Poor More! He was a great tragedy. He always attributed his restraint to me and was, I believe, very bitter against me for it. This is, unfortunately true, for if I had not reported to Alec and Sprigge the condition in which I found him when I visited him at Wotton, Sprigge would never have sent down to have him certified. Sprigge told me later that he himself would have been prepared to certify him on photographs I took of him."[3]

So, Adey was incarcerated for the next 17 or 18 years and I have no evidence that he was visited during that time by any of his erstwhile friends. There is a story that he was visited by a niece and became violent but was easily calmed. The photographs we have appear to show an elderly man having a quiet smoke in his garden with no other indication of what Vyvyan Holland and Squire Sprigge thought they could see. However, two letters from Christopher Millard to his old bibliographical friend Walter Ledger – also known to Adey and apparently a correspondent on bookish matters – give a more understandable reason for Holland's decision. In July 1925 he wrote:

> More Adey is busy moving to London; also he is in very bad health and has recently met with an accident causing serious

> damage to one eye, which probably accounts for the fact that he has not answered you. As a matter of fact I don't think he ever had a copy of the suppressed De Profundis.[4]

Two months before this Reggie Turner had written to Frank Harris that

> More Adey is now an invalid & no one can get anything out of him. He lives in the country & is, I imagine, at the last gasp of intelligence. He was always excentric [sic][5]

Neither Millard nor Turner seem to have had their information first hand, and why Adey should contemplate leaving his beloved house in Wotton for London, with all its memories of Ross, Wilde and a life left behind is not clear. Whatever his reasons, he never made the move, for only six months after his first letter (that is in January 1926) Millard wrote to Ledger:

> You need not spread this: but you must not expect to see More Adey again, nor can you communicate with him. He is quite irresponsible and for many months past has been in a private "home" near Bristol under constant observation and control. Further, I am told that he is suffering from advanced kidney trouble and may not live long. His last letter to me was quite unintelligible.[6]

The reference to "many months" must be an exaggeration; the order under the Lunacy Act for Adey's incarceration was only made on 3 November 1925. Millard's letters give a quite different view of Adey's mental state from the generally accepted one, which comes from a description in Siegfried Sassoon's memoir, *Siegfried's Journey*, and which was not published until 1945. It reads:

> He was a sallow, moody little man with lustreless, dark eyes, who smoked ceaseless cigarettes ... He could be humorous, and even playful, but there was a solitary and frustrated existence behind it all. After the War he retired to a fine old manor house in the west of England – a property which he had inherited as a young man. His oddity then became actively apparent, and for a while he was happy. Having got it into his head that the house contained hidden treasure, he employed a number of workmen to pull the place to pieces. Free cider flowed like water while More Adey gleefully superintended his party of demolitionists, walking about in a long black cloak, with a tame rook perched on his shoulder. No treasure was found, and the poor old lord of the manor was finally removed from the scene to live on for a few years as a certified case of mental derangement.[7]

It is unlikely that Sassoon had direct evidence of any of this; as far as I can establish, he did not visit Wotton during these years. Unfortunately, because the writers of histories of Wotton quoted Sassoon extensively, his view appears to have coloured the "reminiscences" of local people.

But Sassoon's claims fail to support the idea of someone with significant mental health problems prior, perhaps to the second half of 1925. Adey may have believed there was treasure somewhere in the area, but he did not pull the house apart. A hole was dug but this seems to have been to try and reinstate a well that had served the house in the seventeenth century. The house today retains its Georgian panelling throughout the ground floor and shows no sign of having been extensively damaged. Recollections of Wotton residents varied: one suggested that piles of clay further along Adey's Lane meant that digging was in the fields; another thought the focus of Adey's efforts was at Edbrooke House, which, when sold apparently contained thousands of bottles – said to be an obsession of Adey's.

As for the cider, I suspect that any manual labourer in the west of England at that time who wasn't given cider would have downed tools. The black cloak is apparently true but far from unusual; portraits of Ricketts, Shannon and Sturge Moore (all friends of Adey) show each of them wearing similar cloaks. Neither was the rook – or jackdaw in some versions – unusual either. Dickens had his pet raven Grip stuffed after it died from eating lead based paint and Adey's great friend Edward Perry Warren and his partner John Marshall had a pet crow which sat on Marshall's shoulder as he worked.

Two of Adey's interests may have added to the sense of mental instability: archaeology and the supernatural.

It has been suggested that the digging around the house was archaeologically inspired; certainly he donated coins to the British Museum that could have been found in holes around the property. He had a general antiquarian interest, which was reflected in his approach to art history; he also donated early manuscripts to the British Museum.

The supernatural interest is likely to have been inspired, or at least nurtured by Count Stenbock, whose writings on vampires predate Bram Stoker's novel.[8] It is possible that the name Carfax not only reflected the position of the gallery at the meeting of four roads, and a memory of Oxford, but was a nod to Dracula's home at Carfax Abbey. The 1892 edition of *Melmoth the Wanderer*, which Ross and Adey edited, also indicates an interest in the gothic supernatural.

There is no doubt Adey had his eccentricities but the change from the eccentric local squire to a man whom all his friends agreed needed to be incarcerated seems to have been swift and, on the evidence of Millard's letters, to have been accelerated by physical deterioration.

In the early 1920s Adey was still pursuing literary enquiries through the pages of *Notes and Queries*, where he asked for information about "authors of passages found in an imperfect Collection of Miscellanies by Swift, Pope and others" and the identity of 'Philostratus' "who wrote 'Fides Catholica', apparently during the life time of Malthus". As late as May 1925 Adey was writing long, cogent letters on literary matters. A series of these to Osbert Burdett dealt with the possibility of a biography of Robert Ross:

> The subject of some memoir of Robert Ross has been frequently discussed among his friends, mainly among those very much more interested in him than in Oscar Wilde, such as Edmund Gosse, D.S. McColl, Sir Squire Sprigge, Roderick Meiklejohn, Charles Ricketts, Siegfried Sassoon (among the Youth), Alec Ross and me. I have discussed the subject with all of them, and, of course, with Wilde's son. Among these Meiklejohn and I probably best know the Youth, such as Sassoon, of whom you have met some at 40 Half Moon St. The only person who really has any power in the matter is Alec Ross.

Adey promised to keep Burdett informed of any progress, but said:

> For the moment, I have no definite view except that the proposed memoir should have no connection with "Letters of Oscar Wilde to Robert Ross" & should be issued by a different publisher, with designs by some artist such as Charles Ricketts, unless an equally competent modernist can be found among the Youth of Robert Ross's acquaintance.[9]

This suggests that, at a time when Wilde's reputation was recovering strongly, Adey felt Ross was being overshadowed by his more famous friend. Whether it also points to unhappiness with the way the two volumes of letters had been prepared for publication is not clear, although he had not been impressed by the choice of Ethelbert White to illustrate those volumes.

Burdett had written to Adey in large part about a new magazine called *The Beacon*, edited by E R Appleton, which included contributions from a number of Adey's friends including Selwyn Image, Charles Ricketts and Sturge Moore. Adey expressed sympathy with the aims of the magazine and wondered if the editor would accept a piece from "a great personal friend of mine", Joseph Pijoan. Pijoan was a professor of art history at the

With possession of the Principal Residence

WOTTON-UNDER-EDGE, Gloucestershire

About 2 miles from Charfield (L.M.S.R.) and 8 miles from Badminton (G.W.R.)

PARTICULARS, PLAN AND CONDITIONS OF SALE
OF

UNDER-THE-HILL HOUSE

An Attractive Residential Property

situate on the slopes of the Cotswolds close to the picturesque old town of Wotton-under-Edge, together with GARDENS, STABLING, GARDENER'S COTTAGE, VALUABLE ORCHARDING AND PASTURE LAND having a total area of

11a. 3r. 2p.

EDBROOK HOUSE

An Important Residence

occupying an open position in Old Town, and having an EXCELLENT GARDEN TENNIS LAWN, Etc.

TWO COTTAGES IN OLD TOWN

Valuable Accommodation Pasture Land

in Old Town and Coombe Road, having a total area of

24a. 2r. 21p.

MR HENRY KNOWLES

of the firm of

BRUTON, KNOWLES & CO.

Appointed by the Court, is to Sell these Valuable Properties by Auction

At the SWAN HOTEL, WOTTON-UNDER-EDGE

On FRIDAY, 19th MARCH, 1926

At THREE o'clock punctually, in 7 lots

Further Particulars may be had of
A. H. JOTCHAM, Esq., Solicitor, Wotton-under-Edge, Glos.; of Messrs VIZARD, OLDHAM, CROWDER & CASH, Solicitors 51 Lincoln's Inn Fields, London, W.C.; or of the Auctioneers, Albion Chambers, Gloucester.

Fig. 6 The catalogue for the sale of Under-the-Hill House, 1926.

University of Southern California, having recently left Toronto. It is not known how he and Adey became friends, but it may have been through Edward Perry Warren and John Marshall who had for many years been providing American museums with European antiquities. These included the Boston Museum of Fine Arts, where Pijoan had been part of the management commission in the early years of the century. By 1922 Adey described himself as serving "Pijoan as a sort of 'consul'" and was attempting to get a British magazine to reprint Pijoan's "The Spiritual Adventure of Research" from *The Canadian Forum.* [10]

Burdett had clearly asked Adey for his views on the work of Francis Crease, the calligrapher who so influenced Evelyn Waugh and on whom Burdett had contributed an essay to *The Beacon.* But Adey did "not see anything particularly arresting in it, such as we saw in the first drawing by Beardsley that we came across or in one of A.E. Housman's or de la Mare's lyrics, but you and Warren are not only excellent judges, but are in a position to form a much sounder judgment than I am, and that I accept at present."

The period from his significant involvement in literature and art in 1922, to the autumn of 1925 when Adey entered Brislington House Asylum, constituted a rapid decline. Brislington was, incidentally, the asylum where Wilde's friend the artist Frank Miles had died in 1891.

On Friday 19 March 1926 Adey's property was sold at auction.[11] This consisted of Under-the-Hill House, Edbrooke House, cottages and "valuable accommodation lands 36 acres". There were seven lots, the first of which consisted of Under-the-Hill House, gardens, stabling and the gardener's cottage along with "two valuable meadows and a pasture orchard". This lot was bought by Lt.Col. Alfred Irvine for £1,850. He was then resident in Innisfallen, Northern Ireland and apparently bought the house sight unseen. Lt.Col Irvine's children remembered a hole in the floor of the hall where Adey had dug for the well (which would have been outside the original house). The Irvines stayed until 1962, and during World War II one of the bedrooms was used for the care of wounded soldiers. The next owners stayed for a much shorter time and the house stood empty for two years, by which time it had been prey to time, weather and a swarm of bees. In 1972 it was bought by the present owners who began its restoration; it now stands proudly above the town surrounded by beautiful gardens.

The contents of the house were sold in July 1926 by auction[12] and one would assume from the more than 500 lots, including numerous tablecloths, sundry plants, broken china, etc. that the entire contents were there. But closer study shows almost nothing that would not have been there before Adey's birth. Of the listed books only a fifteen volume *Lives of the Saints*, Varley's *Winchester* and Wheeler's *Old English Furniture* were published after 1875. The only pictures in the sale would not have been Adey's choice.

So what had happened to the Beardsleys, the Simeon Solomons, the inscribed first editions of Wilde and others. Adey was by nature a collector and aesthete, but the contents of the house could have belonged to any provincial solicitor. We have seen that Adey's two major Beardsley pictures had already left his possession by the time Ross wrote his book on Beardsley in 1908. Some early manuscripts went to the British Museum. There had been a donation of books (almost certainly his father's as they were largely eighteenth century historical works) and a reference collection of reproductions of pictures from Adey's *Burlington Magazine* days to Bristol University, but these were made by Adey himself in 1921 and 1922.[13] Some relatively recent books in French and German were donated to the Cambridge University Library in 1906.

All this activity suggests Adey was attempting to jettison the past and it may be that Adey himself started disposing of things when he left London; Christopher Millard's Catalogue 1 at Christmas 1919 featured for £21, William Rothenstein's portrait of Alfred Douglas which had belonged to Wilde and which Adey had acquired at Wilde's request from Ernest Leverson.[14] Between them Alec Ross, Christopher Millard and A J A Symons seem to have rounded up the Wilde material; some of this clearly made its way into the 1928 Dulau catalogue of Wilde material. Other items were later sold to G F Sims, the Berkshire bookdealer, who mentioned it in an article in 1984:

> I bought a good deal of this material [letters and manuscripts concerning Wilde] from Julian Symons and catalogued some of it in 1949 and 1950. A J A Symons had purchased many of the items from C.S. Millard (who, under the pen name "Stuart Mason", completed the mammoth bibliography of Oscar Wilde), but other letters and documents of various kinds had been acquired from Lord Alfred Douglas, Walter Ledger and More Adey.[15]

and this variously found its way to the Clark Library, to Mary Hyde and to H Montgomery Hyde (which then went to Mary Hyde) and subsequently to the British Library. More than one person in Wotton believed that Adey's solicitors – Jotcham the successors to the firm in which his father had been

Fig. 7 The main building of Brislington Asylum in the early years of the 20th century.

a partner - had played a less than straightforward role in the disposal of Adey's possessions, but there is no evidence to support that view.

In the years around the time of Adey's move to Brislington, the Bristol *Kelly's Directory* carried a half page advert for:

> Brislington House, Near Bristol, Established 1804
>
> A private mental hospital for the care and treatment of persons of the upper and middle classes of both sexes.
>
> The house is situated on an estate of 200 acres and has extensive pleasure grounds and a farm connected with it. It lies between Bristol and Bath, 3 miles from Bristol Station, and within 21/2 hours journey from London. In addition to the main building there are several villas, completely detached and pleasantly situated in their own grounds, where there is accommodation for suitable cases. Patients can be received without certificates as Voluntary Borders.
>
> For terms and further particulars apply to the Medical Superintendent.

In 1928 the advert became more specific:

> Patients are encouraged to enter the Hospital on the Voluntary basis whenever suitable, but certified patients are also admitted.
>
> The Beeches Brislington, a completely isolated and separate branch of the Hospital, is reserved for the active treatment of curable and early cases of nervous instability of young persons on the most up-to-date principles, under the most favourable conditions. The accommodation is limited to 6 members of both sexes – voluntary boarders only are accepted.
>
> Heath House, Brislington, another similar house, is reserved for the treatment of 12 lady patients suffering from mild and curable states of nervous disorders – as voluntary boarders.
>
> There are two Resident Physicians, assisted by a consulting staff of a leading London Specialist in Neurological and Psychological Medicine, a General Surgeon, a Dental Surgeon and a Pathologist. Terms are from 6gns a week.

Brislington has been described as "the first lunatic asylum in Britain". This is clearly not true, but it was revolutionary when it was opened in 1806 by the Cornish Quaker, Dr Edward Long Fox. He catered for 106 patients; the nobility and the rich being allowed to keep their own servants. Although there was a padded room in the hospital, Fox's treatments were intended to be humane and kindly. Everything was done to protect patients from themselves: furniture was fixed to the floors or walls and all staircases were made of iron to stop fires spreading. There was a bowling green, tennis and cricket for outside entertainment. Inside chess and billiards were played, musical instruments were available and entertainments were regularly staged. There was a private chapel for Church of England patients and Catholics were taken to visit a local church; Catholic and non-conformist priests also visited the hospital.

Fox "was one of the first asylum owners to use a new treatment for the insane known as moral management, moral therapy or moral treatment". Vital to this was the idea that the asylum itself and, in particular, its place in the landscape, formed part of the care of the patients. Thus it was not enough for patients to be in the open air, they had to be able to see the wider landscape. For patients who could not be allowed into the wider grounds there were enclosed "airing courts", and even here portions of the ground were raised to allow them to see over the walls. As Clare Hickman notes[16], the landscape at Brislington reflected the early 19th century fascination with the picturesque. The cottages – intended for richer patients – had ornamental features including barge boards, verandas and walls covered with climbing plants. They were not only practical but served as points of interest for those walking in the grounds.

Other picturesque features included the Cliff-Top walk and the Grotto. This was reached along a path lined with ferns and rocks and consisted of a viewing platform on which was a stone table "enclosed by a horseshoe-shaped bench ornamented by Sarsen stones". This would no doubt have appealed to Adey's antiquarian interests.

Fox's "moral treatment" and the role of landscape within it was thought to have a speedier effect on the well-educated or those of higher social status. Although in the early years there seems to have been no thought of allowing patients to take a practical interest, by Adey's time there were flourishing farming and horticultural activities in the grounds and we can assume, given Adey's previous success in growing flowers and vegetables, that he would have at least taken an interest in their cultivation at Brislington. During the twentieth century the grounds of Brislington regularly played host to the Brislington Flower Show and the North East Somerset Agricultural Show. There was of course no mention of the main function of Brislington House in the advertisements for these events.

In the mid-nineteenth century Brislington had been at the centre of some allegations of mistreatment of patients, including John, the son of the assassinated Prime Minister Spencer Percival. Little came of these allegations, largely because Brislington was no worse than many other asylums and gave the appearance of being a great deal better than some. Complaints about the cost of keeping a patient there were probably justified; shortly after the mid-century the basic charge was £300 a year. One patient complained that for that she got food no better than at a London boarding house which charged £1 15s a week.[17]

From the number of classified adverts in the 1920s, there appears to have been a high turnover of staff at Brislington. When Adey entered the head nurse was Margaret Eveline Carter and Dr James Rutherford the medical superintendent. In 1929 an experienced "mental nurse" was required for night duty at a salary of £45 per annum. The same year an advert appeared for a probationer, "must be willing to attend lectures and to sit for examination of RMPA". The starting salary was £24 per annum "uniform found". Most of the recruitment was for maids and housekeepers, including a "Vegetable Maid with experience". There appear to have been at least three head gardeners during Adey's time, one of which, in the 1930s, was F W Miles FRHS, who wrote the horticultural and gardening articles in the *Western Daily Press* and *Bristol Mirror*. (It can only be coincidence that another F Miles – the painter Frank – had died a patient at Brislington forty years earlier).

We have no record of Adey's time within the Hospital; the only fixed event during his time there was a visit by King George VI in December 1940 as part of a three day tour of the Bristol area to see war damage. When I talked to people in Wotton-under-Edge, one memory (second or third hand) of Adey in his later years in the town was that he thought he was the Queen of Sheba. Accusing someone of thinking they were the Queen of Sheba used to be fairly common for that generation as a sign that they were putting on airs. It seems unlikely that Adey would have applied

Fig. 8 Sir Samuel Squire Sprigge.

the term to himself, but the idea of the Queen of Sheba meeting the King is an interesting one.

One fleeting record we have of Brislington is the national register taken in 1939; this lists 82 patients, of whom 26 were men, including Adey; he therefore began and ended his life in a predominantly female environment.

The mental hospital – affected as were all similar institutions by the coming of the National Health Service – closed in 1952 when the remaining 70 patients were sent elsewhere and it became a hostel for night nurses at Bristol Royal Infirmary. The "several villas" have now for the most part disappeared; the main house has been turned into flats and is Grade 1 listed. On the other side of the main road is a park and ride car park.

A letter from Vyvyan Holland to Reggie Turner in 1935 says that Squire Sprigge had told him that Adey was "fading fast".[18] Not that fast it would seem because he did not die until January 1942. There was a brief obituary in the *Times*, although there was a lot going on in the world at the time and a short notice was all that could be expected. The death certificate gave the cause of death as "senile decay and influenza". He was eighty three years old.

The dating of Vyvyan Holland's letter may explain why the catalogue of the William Andrews Clark Library for many years resolutely gave Adey's death date as 1935.

By the time Adey died all his sisters were dead: Ellen and Winifred had died just over a month apart in December 1928 and January 1929. His will, made in 1919 had left everything to them and had not been amended. If the cost of staying at Brislington for seventeen years was taken from the proceeds of the sale of Under the Hill House and its contents, it is surprising that there was anything left to leave them by this time anyway. But he left £4,320 6s 7d gross, and letters of administration were granted to his nephew Vyvian Clarke, the son of Adey's sister Amy Constance, who had married Walter Clarke, a bank manager. Vyvian Clarke was a newsagent and tobacconist in Brighton. Amy had died in 1938.

One of the mysteries about Adey has been where he is buried. His father and mother and one sister are buried in the churchyard of St Mary's in Wotton-under-Edge and I believed Adey would have wanted to be buried close to his mother or perhaps to Ross. However, his death in Brislington and the fact of his Catholicism made that unlikely. He died in the middle of a World War and had no close surviving family, so it is unlikely that his wishes would have been known or could have been acted upon. But he was returned to the town cemetery in Wotton-under-Edge. The ground in the cemetery is very soft and there are very many unmarked graves. Adey was buried in plot 136 but almost all the numbers have disappeared and the lack of memorials makes it difficult to know whether a grave exists or not. The photograph reproduced here shows the row in which plot 136 should be. A sad conclusion to seventeen sad years.

Notes

1 *The Times* of 2 December 1908 carried a full report of the evening. Adey was not mentioned in the highly selective list of those present. There were oddities in the seating arrangements: for example Ricketts was next to Roger Fry, with Cyril Holland across the table about as far from Ross as possible.

2 Adey to Burnett, 3 May 1922. Private collection.

3 Holland to Turner, 14 August 1935, William Andrews Clark Library.

4 Millard to Ledger 7 July 1925, University College Oxford; and yet it was only in May that Adey had written to Millard about Stenbock and Scandinavian literature, giving advice on what Millard should be putting away for future profit. One of the books he suggested was by the man who, shortly thereafter, was to sign the papers committing Adey to an asylum. *Odd Issues*, Squire Sprigge, Leonard Smithers 1899. The first story in the collection, 'Mr Bonnamy's Bishopric' probably appealed to Adey as it concerns a "disciple of Balzac" who is writing "the English *Comédie Humaine*"

5 Turner to Harris, 16 May 1925, University of Texas

6 Millard to Ledger 21 January 1926, University College Oxford

7 *Siegfried's Journey*, Siegfried Sassoon, Faber and Faber 1945, p. 35

8 Stenbock's story 'The True Story of a Vampire' was published in his *Studies of Death*, David Nutt 1894. Bram Stoker's *Dracula* was published by Constable in 1897

9 Adey to Burdett, 3 May 1922. Private collection

10 Adey to Burdett, 19 September and 27 September 1922. Private collection

11 The sale was conducted by Mr Henry Knowles of Bruton, Knowles & Co, estate agents of Gloucester. The front of the catalogue is headed: "53 Vic. c. 5 and Amending Acts/ In the matter of William More Adey, Pursuant to the Order under S. 116, s.s.1. (c) dated 3rd November 1925". This is a reference to the Lunacy Act and would therefore have made clear to everyone that Adey

had been – in modern terms – sectioned. The wording was repeated in the advertisement for the sale which appeared in the *Gloucester Journal* on the previous Saturday.

12 The sale, over two days was conducted by John E Pritchard & Co of Bristol. The lots were described as being "The Property of the Adey Family" with no mention of More Adey. The catalogue contained photographs of a few of the better items of furniture.

13 The "gift of photographs and prints" was reported in the *Western Daily Press* of 24 February 1921; they would "form a valuable supplement to the "Sturge Collection," illustrating European Art and Architecture". Two "Clifton ladies" were arranging and cataloguing them, but they did not, unfortunately, differentiate Adey's gift in their cataloguing so it is not possible to say which images he donated.

14 *The Complete Letters of Oscar Wilde,* edited by Rupert Hart-Davis and Merlin Holland, Fourth Estate 2000. A note on p. 564 says of this drawing "This one, entitled *The Editor of the Spirit Lamp at work,* showed him in profile, wearing flannels and lying back in an armchair. It was commissioned by Wilde and later came into the possession of More Adey. Its present whereabouts are unknown." While Wilde was in prison the picture, along with the portrait of Wilde by Harper Pennington were left with Ernest Leverson. Wilde requested that Adey retrieve them and keep them for him but Wilde's removal to France meant they were never collected. The drawing is now understood to be in a private collection in the USA.

15 'Son of Oscar Wilde" by George Sims in *Antiquarian Book Monthly Review,* Vol XI, No 2, Issue 118, February 1984

16 Clare Hickman, "The Picturesque at Brislington House, Bristol: the Role of Landscape in Relation to the Treatment of Mental Illness in the Early Nineteenth-Century Asylum" in *Garden History: Journal of the Garden History Society,* Vol 33, No 1, Summer 2005.

17 Much fascinating detail about Brislington's early history can be found in *Inconvenient People: Lunacy, Liberty and the Mad Doctors in Victorian England,* Sarah Wise, The Bodley Head, 2012. As the advert for 1928 states that terms were from 6 guineas a week, rates had apparently not risen significantly in sixty years.

18 Holland to Turner op cit.

INDEX

THE RIVENDALE PRESS

RIVENDALE PRESS
P. O. Box 85, High Wycombe, Bucks HP14 4WZ United Kingdom
www.rivendalepress.com

THE LIST OF THE RIVENDALE PRESS

Specialist Publisher of Studies in Turn-of-the-Century British Literature and Culture

ATKINSON (DAMIAN), ed.

The Letters of William Ernest Henley to Robert Louis Stevenson. £40/$65.

Atkinson's edition of these letters, many published here for the first time and enhanced by excellent introductions and extensive notes, is an important contribution to further understanding the Henley-Stevenson relationship. The editor presents a Henley who is astute yet with considerable foibles, an influential man of letters who fostered the careers of many writers of his time, and whose own literary accomplishments deserve our attention.
From: Todd Avery. "Book Reviews." *English Literature in Transition 1880-1920* (53.3, 2010)

ALLISON (JONATHAN), ed.

Bound for the 1890s: Essays on Writing and Publishing in Honor of James G. Nelson. With a preface by G. Thomas Tanselle.
£30/$55.

Bound for the 1890s accomplishes that often elusive goal in a collection of essays penned by diverse hands. While remaining historically and thematically coherent, it affords fresh perspectives on a number of familiar (and some less familiar) 1890s figures. The essays in this volume would not have been possible without the pioneering scholarship of James G. Nelson, and by building on that scholarship, its contributors admirably illustrate book history's manifold critical and scholarly possibilities.
From: Gregory Mackie. "Book Reviews." *The Journal of Pre-Raphaelite Studies.*

COHEN (PHILIP)

John Evelyn Barlas, A Critical Biography: Poetry, Anarchism, and Mental Illness in Late-Victorian Britain.
£40/$65.

John Evelyn Barlas (1860-1914). Nineties poet and anarchist, will very likely have no other biography than this appealing and thoroughly documented life-and-works by Philip K. Cohen. ... Shortly before his death he wrote to Henry Salt, who had published some of his verse in *Songs of Freedom* (1893): "There are now about 25 full blown dramas & 20 vols. of Lyrics besides novels & other things. But scarcely anything issued [in print]." All we have is Philip Cohen's fascinating book bringing Barlas back to his wasted life..
From: Stanley Weintraub. "Book Reviews." *English Literature in Transition 1880-1920.*

COUSTILLAS (PIERRE)

George Gissing: The Definitive Bibliography.
£75/$110.

It is the largest and by far the best enquiry ever conducted into the fascinating history of Gissing's works. It is the result of an extraordinary research effort over more than forty years, and it meets a long-felt need. It offers definitive exactness and evidence across a very considerable range of relevant and essential material. And it is much more than a bibliography. ... The work is both [sic] literary, critical, and historical. It offers an extensive study both of the books and of the manuscripts, which have been inspected when extant and where traced. It provides detailed information about the human and historical processes of composition and publication, and scholarly insight into the entire cultural context of the making of books in late-Victorian England. ... "Coustillas on Gissing" will remain for many years ahead the atlas of the Gissing world. It makes a major contribution to our understanding of the workings of the Victorian book trade and its impact on the wider culture. ...In addition to descriptions of the books Coustillas offers important material concerned with the physical and the psychic form of the book, with concepts of authorship, with the conditions of authorial agency, and with the reading process in a wider evolving culture. This is fine wine, truthfully labeled, and in a handsome bottle too.
From: John Spiers. "Book Reviews." *English Literature in Transition 1880-1920.*

COSTE (BÉNÉDICTE) & DELYFER (CATHERINE), eds.

Aesthetic Lives: 'New experiences, new subjects of poetry, new forms of art'.
£30/$45.

EELLS (EMILLY), ed.

Two *Tombeaux* to Oscar Wilde: Jean Cocteau's *Dorian Gray* and Raymond Laurent's essay on Wildean aesthetics.

£40/$65.

FRANKEL (NICHOLAS), ed.

Charles Ricketts, *Everything For Art*: Selected Writings.

£40/$65.

... succeeds in recovering for current scholars this important aesthete of the fin de siècle, proving him to be not only the great book designer and illustrator many know, but also a significant art historian and critic. It is certainly an important book for students of book history and design. It is useful for anyone working on the 1890s, Oscar Wilde, Michael Field, and the Decadence. It is vital for those interested in Ricketts and the circles in which he moved.
From: Sharon Aronoesky Weltman *English Literature in Transition 1880-1920.* (58:4 2015)

FRANKEL (NICHOLAS)

Masking The Text: Essays on Literature & Mediation in the 1890s.

£40/$65.

Essays on 1890s Print Culture: Volume 2

Frankel's superb essays on British literature of the 1890s are eclectic. Divided into two parts, "Mediating the Text" and "Literature and the Medium of the Book," the collection covers subjects ranging from Oscar Wilde, Michael Field, George Meredith, Aubrey Beardsley, and James McNeill Whistler to William Morris, the Rhymers Club, collecting, forgery, typography, and the literary ramifications of the typewriter. Frankel is preoccupied with the belief that readers "have much to learn from a remarkable body of work from the early 1890s attesting to the truth of masks and the importance of dress for illusion." He brilliantly interweaves critical and textual theory, the history of the book, literary criticism, study of print media, aesthetics, and history. Particularly noteworthy chapters include "The Typewritten Self: Media Technology and Identity in Oscar Wilde's De Profundis ," "James McNeill Whistler and the Politics of the Page," and "Poem, Book, Habitat: The World of George Meredith's Poetry" (the last a rare account). Well produced and bound, and including 39 interesting illustrations and spine and front-cover design, this book should be in every collection on this period. Summing Up: Highly recommended.
From: William Baker. *Choice.*

Frankel is an authoritative representative of yet another tradition that has embraced the reinvigorated study of the book as an alternative sequel to the theoretical death of the author. For Frankel, all critics ought to be, to some

extent, bibliographers of a certain kind. and this claim would seem to have a particular urgency for scholars of the Victorian period and its purported culmination in the 1890s.
From: William R. McKelvy. *Victorian Studies*

HALLIWELL (STEVEN)
Fifty Years of Hand-Printing: A Bibliography of the Tragara Press.
£30/$55.

Also a special edition limited in number with a hand-printed poem, enclosed in a slip case.

[Out of print.

HOLMES (JOHN) & DISTILLER (NATASHA), eds.
Horae Amoris: The Collected Poems of Rosa Newmarch.
£40/$65.

LASNER (MARK SAMUELS)
The Bookplates of Aubrey Beardsley.
£12.50/$25.

Learned, informative, and as comprehensive as the present state of knowledge allows, Mark Samuels Lasner's book is a must-have for students of the fin-de-siècle literature and the book arts, and will also form a welcome addition to the shelves of bibliophiles and book collectors.
From: Lorraine Janzen Kooistra. *The Journal of Pre-Raphaelite Studies*

[Out of print.

LASNER (MARK SAMUELS)
A Bibliography of Enoch Soames (1862-1897).
£20/$35.

Mark Samuels Lasner's *A Bibliography of Enoch Soames (1862-1897)*, with its afterward by Margaret D. Stetz, is a superb work of reconstructive creative bibliography. Hopefully Lasner and The Rivendale Press will make Enoch Soames' poems available!
From: William Baker. "Book Reviews." *Analytical and Enumerative Bibliography.*

O'MAHONY (CLAIRE), ed.

Symbolist Objects: Materiality and Subjectivity at the Fin-de-Siècle. £40/$65.

Only relatively recently have art historians and literary scholars begin to chart the Symbolist fascination with materialism, both in the works themselves and in the larger sense of their connection with the broader consumer culture of the fin de siècle. In exploring this subject, Mahoney and her contributors have revealed the intriguing paradox at the heart of Symbolism: a movement obsessed with suggestion, symbol, and the realm of the ideal was also the first one to elevate form, the very thingness of the object, to the highest realm.
From: Laura Morowitz. *Nineteenth-Century Art Worldwide*

PINNEY (THOMAS) & RICHARDS (DAVID ALAN)

Kipling and His First Publisher: Correspondence of Rudyard Kipling with Thacker, Spink and Co. £30/$55.

None but the most devoted student of the publications of Thacker, Spink, and Company will know of this short work, so we do not hesitate to draw to attention a collaboration by a contributor to the previous issue of PBSA. Thacker, Spink, and Company, Calcutta, were the publishers of Kipling's first two books, *Departmental Ditties* and *Plain Tales from the Hills*; the letters describe their publication in some detail.
From: T. H. Howard-Hill. "Short Notices." *Papers of The Bibliographic Society of America.*

PROPAS (SHARON)

Victorian Studies: A Research Guide.
£30/$55.
(New and updated edition)

NELSON (JAMES G.)

A Checklist of Early Bodley Head Books: 1889-1894.
£25/$45.

[A] volume of serious, specialized scholarship undertaken by the foremost authority on the most prestigious publishing house that brought out the works of so many nineties figures. . . . Sooner or later, most devotees of the 1890s will want to consult this Bodley Head checklist.
From: G. A. Cevasco. "Book Reviews." *English Literature in Transition 1880-1920*

NELSON (JAMES G.)

Publisher to the Decadents: Leonard Smithers in the Careers of Beardsley, Wilde, Dowson.

£25.

(Published in the United States by Penn State University Press)

We see how the authors' circumstances interact with the creative process; how a skillful, if uxorious, publisher supports, prompts, and cajoles his artists in often distressing circumstances; and how type, paper, binding materials, illustration, and title-page design combine in masterpieces of the publisher's art... . Publisher to the Decadents will satisfy the most rigorous scholar. But it will also engage the general reader with an interest in Wilde, Beardsley, or Dowson, the decadent 1890s, or publishing history."
From: Phillip K. Cohen. *Albion*

SCHWARZ (ARTHUR L.)

Dear Mr. Cockerell, Dear Mr. Peirce: The Correspondence of Sir Sydney Cockerell and Harold Peirce in the Grolier Club Archive.

£30/$55.

This pioneering and detailed summary of a long correspondence adds substantially to knowledge of a world much of which had to be conducted in private.
From: David McKitterick. *The Times Literary Supplement*

SEENEY (MICHAEL)

From Bow Street to the Ritz: Oscar Wilde's Theatrical Career from 1895 to 1908.

£12.50/$20.

"What I love about the book is that it tells a story we didn't know – and it's full of surprises. Beautifully researched and illustrated, elegantly and entertainingly written, this is a must-read for anyone interested in Wilde and late Victorian and Edwardian theatre"
Gyles Brandreth.

SEENEY (MICHAEL)

More Adey: Oscar Wilde's Forgotten Friend.

£12.50/$20.

[Immediately.

SHEPPARD (DARREN J.)

Theodore Wratislaw: Fragments of a Life.

£40/$65.

...It is this aspect of Sheppard's study – the careful detailing of artistic networks in 1890's London – that, I think, offers the most valuable insights. Creating art was important, of course, but knowing which cafes to frequent, and which critics to attract the attention of, was obviously crucial. Wratislaw's best review, notably, was written by one of his closest friends; he used his own reviews, meanwhile, as a means of getting back at his enemies (Richard La Gallienne being an especial target). In fact, Wratislaw received very few reviews – and probably sold very little work – outside of his own circles. Only one of his publications (his study of Swinburne) made it into a second edition, and most were self-funded in part, if not in whole. His literary career was a struggle, with few obvious rewards, save a passing mention in a literary study or two (and popularity among collectors for whom the rarity of Wratislaw's publications makes him all the more interesting). Sheppard recounts these struggles with great patience and authority, and a keen understanding of the wider context of the poet's endeavours.

Wratislaw was – like most of his peers – unlucky to have been part of a movement that was essentially killed off overnight, following the social uproar over Wilde's trial. In this book, however, he has proved himself very lucky indeed: few marginal figures get such meticulous treatment, despite the light such studies shed on wider questions of the period. This is not only a marvellously-detailed book, but a beautifully-produced one too: much more than the sum of the fragments it purports to present.

From: Samuel Shaw. *The Edwardian Network*

SÖDER (HANS-PETER)

That Way Madness Lies: Max Nordau on Fin-de-Siècle Genius.

£40/$65.

STETZ (MARGARET D.)

Gender and the London Theatre, 1880–1920.

£30/$55.

(Published in association with Bryn Mawr College Library)

The book is the product of an exhibition held at Bryn Mawr College Library, and serves as a wonderfully detailed catalogue to that exhibition, as well as replicating many of its images for those of us not fortunate enough to see the exhibition in 2003. ... To describe this book as only a catalogue, however, does it an injustice. It opens with a substantial introduction by Stetz, which offers an engaging survey of part of the theatre industry in the 1890s, focusing on the theatrical activities of writers and artists perhaps better known in other fields, such as George Moore. The book is lavishly illustrated and

includes detailed and perceptive notes on each image. …
From: Katharine Newey. "Book Reviews." *Victorian Studies.*

STETZ (MARGARET D.) & CHERYL A. WILSON, eds.
Michael Field and Their World.
£30/$55.

[*Very few remain.*

Michael Field and Their World grew out of a 2004 conference on the Michael Fields… While the editors clearly hope that the collection will have crossover appeal to a broad range of readers — for example, people interested in gender identity, conversion, and dogs — few if any readers will find all the essays of interest as Stetz and Wilson acknowledge. Nevertheless, if viewed as an initial attempt to define some of the issues that will occupy scholars and students of the poets and their lives, the collection can indeed be seen as productively "ground-breaking."
From: Stefanie Markovits. "Book Reviews." *English Literature in Transition 1880-1920*

… I want also to note that this collection of essays is beautifully designed by Mark Samuels Lasner, one of the organisers of the 2004 conference, and its own material form elevates the dialogic and reflective experience of reading its contents. The diverse approach represented here should engage current readers and scholars and attract new ones to the works of Michael Field, which like these essays, will remain compelling, paradoxical, and important.
From: Natalie M. Houston. "Book Reviews." *The Journal of Pre-Raphaelite Studies.*

STURGIS (MATTHEW)
Masks and Phases.
£20/$30.

[*Out of Print.*

WHITTINGTON-EGAN (MOLLY)
Frank Miles and Oscar Wilde: "such white lilies".
£12.50/$25.

WHITTINGTON-EGAN (RICHARD)

Stephen Phillips: A Biography.

£30/$55.

Whittington-Egan writes the first biography of poet and dramatist Stephen Phillips (1864-1915). Only a few scholars of the period today would know that Phillips blazed across the scene in the 1890s and then quickly fell into obscurity.

From: "Book Reviews." *English Literature in Transition 1880-1920* (50.3, 2007)

WILKINSON (DAVID)

'Guy Thorne': C. Ranger Gull - Edwardian Tabloid Novelist and His Unseemly Brotherhood.

£40/$65

Gull's immense popularity and influence during the Edwardian period make him an important figure to be rescued from the proverbial dustbin of history and we can be grateful to David Wilkinson for admirably beginning the task.'

From: Bethany Kilcrease, Aquinas College, Grand Rapids, MI

WILKINSON (DAVID)

Arthur Greening: That Damned Elusive Publisher

£40/$65

FIN